Modern Brazil: A Very Short Introduction

VERY SHORT INTRODUCTIONS are for anyone wanting a stimulating and accessible way into a new subject. They are written by experts, and have been translated into more than 45 different languages.

The series began in 1995, and now covers a wide variety of topics in every discipline. The VSI library currently contains over 650 volumes—a Very Short Introduction to everything from Psychology and Philosophy of Science to American History and Relativity—and continues to grow in every subject area.

Very Short Introductions available now:

ABOLITIONISM Richard S. Newman
THE ABRAHAMIC RELIGIONS
    Charles L. Cohen
ACCOUNTING Christopher Nobes
ADAM SMITH Christopher J. Berry
ADOLESCENCE Peter K. Smith
ADVERTISING Winston Fletcher
AERIAL WARFARE Frank Ledwidge
AESTHETICS Bence Nanay
AFRICAN AMERICAN RELIGION
    Eddie S. Glaude Jr
AFRICAN HISTORY John Parker and
    Richard Rathbone
AFRICAN POLITICS Ian Taylor
AFRICAN RELIGIONS
    Jacob K. Olupona
AGEING Nancy A. Pachana
AGNOSTICISM Robin Le Poidevin
AGRICULTURE Paul Brassley and
    Richard Soffe
ALBERT CAMUS Oliver Gloag
ALEXANDER THE GREAT
    Hugh Bowden
ALGEBRA Peter M. Higgins
AMERICAN BUSINESS HISTORY
    Walter A. Friedman
AMERICAN CULTURAL HISTORY
    Eric Avila
AMERICAN FOREIGN RELATIONS
    Andrew Preston
AMERICAN HISTORY Paul S. Boyer
AMERICAN IMMIGRATION
    David A. Gerber
AMERICAN LEGAL HISTORY
    G. Edward White

AMERICAN NAVAL HISTORY
    Craig L. Symonds
AMERICAN POLITICAL HISTORY
    Donald Critchlow
AMERICAN POLITICAL PARTIES
    AND ELECTIONS L. Sandy Maisel
AMERICAN POLITICS
    Richard M. Valelly
THE AMERICAN PRESIDENCY
    Charles O. Jones
THE AMERICAN REVOLUTION
    Robert J. Allison
AMERICAN SLAVERY
    Heather Andrea Williams
THE AMERICAN WEST
    Stephen Aron
AMERICAN WOMEN'S HISTORY
    Susan Ware
ANAESTHESIA Aidan O'Donnell
ANALYTIC PHILOSOPHY
    Michael Beaney
ANARCHISM Colin Ward
ANCIENT ASSYRIA Karen Radner
ANCIENT EGYPT Ian Shaw
ANCIENT EGYPTIAN ART AND
    ARCHITECTURE Christina Riggs
ANCIENT GREECE Paul Cartledge
THE ANCIENT NEAR EAST
    Amanda H. Podany
ANCIENT PHILOSOPHY Julia Annas
ANCIENT WARFARE
    Harry Sidebottom
ANGELS David Albert Jones
ANGLICANISM Mark Chapman
THE ANGLO-SAXON AGE John Blair

For more information visit our website

www.oup.com/vsi/

Anthony W. Pereira

MODERN BRAZIL

A Very Short Introduction

OXFORD
UNIVERSITY PRESS

OXFORD
UNIVERSITY PRESS

Great Clarendon Street, Oxford, OX2 6DP,
United Kingdom

Oxford University Press is a department of the University of Oxford.
It furthers the University's objective of excellence in research, scholarship,
and education by publishing worldwide. Oxford is a registered trade mark of
Oxford University Press in the UK and in certain other countries

First edition published in 2020

Impression: 1

Published in the United States of America by Oxford University Press
198 Madison Avenue, New York, NY 10016, United States of America

British Library Cataloguing in Publication Data
Data available

Library of Congress Control Number: 2020936018

ISBN 978-0-19-881208-1

Printed in Great Britain by
Ashford Colour Press Ltd, Gosport, Hampshire

To Rita, Bela, Bevan, and Sagwa, our indomitable Recife-born cat

Contents

Acknowledgements

The list of people that I should thank, after many years of visiting, living and teaching in, researching and writing about Brazil is too long to include in this short book. But I would be remiss not to give thanks to some people. Since 2010 I have had the good fortune to be Director of the Brazil Institute at King's College London. My former Vice Principal Keith Hoggart and colleagues Leslie Bethell, Jeff Garmany, and Sónia Gonçalves taught me much and were a pleasure to work with. The Brazil Institute's affiliated faculty, students, and Senior Advisory Board, as well as the faculty and students of the Department of International Development and the School of Global Affairs at King's College London, have been generous with me in sharing their views about some of the issues analysed in this book. I have also been lucky to have exchanged ideas with colleagues working on Brazil at other UK universities, including Tim Power, Andreza de Souza Santos, Mahrukh Doctor, Fiona Macaulay, Par Engstrom, Marco Vieira, Malu Gatto, Kathryn Hochstetler, Francisco Panizza, Sacha Dark, Gareth Jones, Alex Shankland, Roxana Cavalcanti, Linda Newson, Graham Denyer Willis, and Ana Margheritis. I would also like to thank my Brazil Institute colleague Vinicius Carvalho for accepting the challenge of guiding the Brazil Institute into its second decade.

The University of São Paulo's International Relations Institute has been the Brazil Institute's partner for almost ten years and my academic home on several occasions. The faculty and students there received me warmly, sharing their passion for researching the connections between Brazil's domestic politics and its role in the world. I have been helped in particular by IRI's Janina Onuki, Amâncio Oliveira, Pedro Feliú, Alexandre Moreli, Alvaro Comin, Cristiane Lucena Carneiro, Felipe Loureiro, Kai Lehmann, Leandro Piquet, Maria Hermínia Tavares de Almeida, Pedro Dallari, Rafael Villa, Vinicius Rodrigues Vieira, and Adriana Schor. I was also a visitor at the Centre for Research on and Documentation of the Contemporary History of Brazil (CPDOC) at the Getúlio Vargas Foundation (FGV) in Rio de Janeiro where Celso Castro, Paulo Fontes, Marco Aurélio Vannucchi, and Américo Freire were friendly, interested, and interesting colleagues. Vicente Arruda Câmara Rodrigues and Heliene Nagasava were expert guides for me in the National Archive in Rio. Colleagues in the Political Science departments of the Federal University of Pernambuco and the Federal University of Minas Gerais, where I was a short-term visitor, include Marcelo Medeiros, Ernani Carvalho, Jorge Zaverucha, Leonardo Avritzer, and Mario Fuchs. Other Brazil-based scholars who have helped me in my attempts to understand the intricacies of modern Brazil's history, politics, economy, and foreign policy include Matias Spektor, Eduardo Mello, Cecilia Mariz, Lauro Mattei, Bruno Konder Comparato, Marta Arretche, Juliana Martins, Ursula Dias Peres, Rubens Ricupero, Bernardo Ricupero, Jairo Nicolau, Flávia Biroli, Tânia Pellegrini, João Roberto Martins Filho, Paulo Sérgio Pinheiro, Sergio Adorno, Maria Celina D'Araújo, David Fleischer, the late Terrie Groth, Loussia Musse Felix, Emílio Neder Meyer, and Maria do Socorro Sousa Braga. Scholars based in the United States, such as Chris Dunn, Idelber Avelar, Aaron Schneider, Rafael Ioris, Leila Lehnen, Rebecca Atencio, Bryan McCann, Jerry Dávila, and Jeff Lesser, have also shared their work and insights with me.

Evgeny Dunaev conducted valuable research assistance for this book, and Bela Pereira did the index. Vinicius Carvalho, Michael Hall, Alfredo Saad-Filho, Matt Taylor, and Jairo Nicolau commented on all or parts of the manuscript. Two anonymous reviewers for Oxford University Press reviewed the initial proposal and two others commented on the first draft of the manuscript. The VSI series' senior commissioning editor Andrea Keegan set me on course for writing this book, and her colleague Jenny Nugee helped me with her patience and practical good sense in guiding me towards the completion of the manuscript. As is usual in these cases, all remaining errors of fact and interpretation in the book are my exclusive responsibility.

List of illustrations

Modern Brazil

Chapter 1
Brazil hosts the Olympic Games

Brazil: we've all been there, whether we've actually visited the country or not. The landmarks of Rio de Janeiro, such as the Christ the Redeemer statue, Sugarloaf mountain, and Copacabana beach are instantly recognizable. In addition to these images, Brazil is associated in many people's minds with conviviality, sensuality, beautiful bodies, and spectacular nature, including the largest tropical rainforest in the world, the Amazon, almost two-thirds of which is Brazilian. We all know Brazil, and many of us love it.

At the same time, the country behind these images and associations is something of an enigma. This is despite the fact that it is the fifth largest country in the world in terms of territory (smaller only than Russia, Canada, China, and the United States), the sixth largest in terms of population, with over 210 million people (smaller only than India, China, the United States, Indonesia, and Pakistan), and one of the world's ten largest national economies. Brazil is alternately praised as a 'country of the future', a rising power ready to take its place at the top tables of global governance, and written off as a perennial disappointment, a country failing to reach its potential, mired in corruption, inequality, poverty, and violence. These oscillations between euphoria and despair obscure a country with its own unique trajectory to the 21st century, a continental-sized bundle of contradictions, a pluralistic, fast-changing country with complicated political conflicts, ethno-racial mixture, and cultural synergy.

One way to understand Brazil's complexity is to examine its civic rituals, occasions in which the political establishment represents the nation to its own citizens and the wider world. Such rituals are stage-managed by powerful economic and political elites, but they often depict widely shared visions of the nation. One such occasion was the opening ceremony of the 2016 Olympic Games in Rio de Janeiro on 5 August 2016, put on by Rio2016, the Organizing Committee for the Rio Olympics. This ceremony is worth examining in some detail, even though the government of that time was succeeded in 2019 by a new one that would probably have organized a very different event.

This was the first time the games took place in South America, and the opening ceremony was watched live by hundreds of millions of people around the world, as well as 80,000 in the Maracanã stadium. The four-hour ceremony tells us something about Brazil and its national experience. It also provides insights into what makes Brazilians proud to be Brazilian, as well as anxieties behind those sources of pride. The themes concern nature, the future, peaceful inclusion, and informality.

Bountiful nature

The first and dominant theme of the ceremony was the importance of nature and its preservation. These were declared the 'green games of Rio'. An image of a tree in the form of a peace sign was projected onto the stadium floor accompanied by the words 'Reinvent, Rejoice, Replant' (see Figure 1). The Brazilian flag was then raised by the environmental police of Rio, while the musician Paulinho da Viola, with an acoustic guitar, performed an

1. The opening ceremony of the Rio Olympic Games on 5 August 2016.

understated version of the national anthem. Many in the stadium sang along. The anthem proclaims that Brazil is a 'gentle mother . . . lying eternally in a splendid cradle', blessed with a nature that is both beautiful and rich in natural resources. The anthem's lyrics state, 'Our fields have more flowers' and 'Our forests have more life', and scientific research confirms that Brazil is home to an immense array of biodiversity, with an estimated 50,000 plant species in the Amazon basin alone. Even the name of the country comes from a tree, *pau brasil*, that was cut down and exported to Europe to make red dye during the early days of Portuguese colonial rule.

Throughout the ceremony, there were many other evocations of this environmental theme. When the time came for the athletes to parade into the stadium, each of them had been given a cartridge with a seed. The athletes placed these cartridges in mirrored towers located in the stadium. The idea was that 24 million trees would be planted to offset the carbon emissions produced as a

3

result of hosting the games. In the Athletes' Forest in the Radical Park of Deodoro, in the western part of Rio, 207 species of tree, one for each competing delegation, would grow. A recording of the Brazilian actress Fernanda Montenegro and the British actress Judi Dench included this message: 'It is not sufficient to stop damaging the planet, it is the time to start to heal it. This will be our Olympic message: Earthlings, let's replant, let's save the planet!'

This leads to the question: can Brazil preserve its environment and help save the planet? The messages are mixed. Over 500 years, the vast majority of the coastal Atlantic rainforest was destroyed. Almost 20 per cent of the Amazon rainforest in Brazil has gone in only a few decades. The rate of deforestation declined by 80 per cent between 2004 and 2012, and Brazil has a relatively clean energy matrix, with heavy reliance on renewables such as hydro and biofuels. But deforestation in the Amazon has crept back up since 2012, and the rate of deforestation between 1 August 2018 and 31 July 2019 was an increase of 30 per cent over the year before. Perhaps more worrying than the rate, which is still below the level before 2004, is that the government that started its mandate in 2019 seems to view environmental preservation as an obstacle to development, and prefers the latter to the former.

Scientists believe that as deforestation proceeds, there will be a tipping point at which the rest of the Amazon rainforest will not have enough water to survive, and the whole forest could decline. The tipping point could be as close as 25 per cent of the forest, a point not that far away. It is not clear that patterns of Brazilian economic growth will change quickly enough to avoid the destruction of much of the natural environment that provides Brazil with its beauty and biodiversity. Perhaps tellingly, when it came to planting trees, the Rio organizers did not meet their target. Only a fraction of the 24 million trees was actually planted, and some died for lack of care afterwards.

A country of the future?

Another theme emphasized by the opening ceremony was the importance of the future in Brazilians' view of the world. When Paulinho de Viola played the national anthem, he sat on a platform that evoked the curved lines drawn by Oscar Niemeyer, the Brazilian architect who designed the UN's headquarters in New York City and many of the official buildings in Brasília, including the national Congress. These buildings, constructed in the mid-20th century, were intended to evoke modernity. Brasília, the new capital of Brazil built from scratch and inaugurated in 1960, is full of Niemeyer's work and can be considered the spiritual home of futuristic high modernism in South America, in the same way that Machu Picchu in Peru is the spiritual home of the pre-Colombian era in the region. The creation of Brasília was part of an aspiration to show the world the capacity of Brazil to innovate and help lead the way to a better human future.

This embrace of modernity, the forward-looking and optimistic stance, is based at least in part on a desire to overcome and redeem a troubled history of human exploitation and economic dependence. For more than 300 years, Brazil was a slave-owning society, forcibly importing millions of human beings from Africa to work on its plantations and in its mines. In the 19th century it was the largest slave-owning society in the world, and it was the last in the western hemisphere to abolish slavery, doing so only in 1888. For some observers such as the sociologist Jessé Souza, Brazil has yet to transcend the social divisions caused by slavery.

One of the compelling ideas about Brazil is that it could become a country better than its origins. A former slave society could become a social democracy, embedding markets in institutions of social protection and creating an equality of citizenship. This is an idea that has been shared by some foreign observers. In 1941 the novelist and essayist Stefan Zweig published a rather fanciful book called *Brazil: A Land of the Future*. Zweig, a Jew from Austria, had escaped the Nazis and arrived in Brazil in 1940. For Zweig, many characteristics of Brazilian society stood in stark and healthy contrast to the militarism and ethno-nationalism of Europe in the 1930s. He saw in Brazil a country of peace that was showing Europe how racial mixture and tolerance could work in a large-scale society. But what if outsiders, the more than 97 per cent of the world's population who are not Brazilian, never recognize Brazil's contributions to modernity? What if the cruel jibe that Brazil is 'the country of the future, and always will be', is true?

Brazilians sometimes fear that their contributions to modernity will be neglected by the outside world, that they will forever be stereotyped as a land where nature and the eternal pleasures and pains of the body predominate over science, rationality, and progress. This can be seen in their reverence for the Brazilian aviation pioneer Alberto Santos Dumont, who was depicted in the opening ceremony of the Olympic Games in the cockpit of his biplane as it took off from Maracanã stadium and flew over Rio's southern beach neighbourhoods of Copacabana, Ipanema, and Leblon. This was a somewhat exaggerated depiction of the plane—it never flew that far or that high—but it reminded a worldwide audience that Santos Dumont had a claim to have made the first flight by a heavier-than-air machine.

Santos Dumont was born in 1873 in a town in the interior of Brazil that now bears his name. In 1906 he made two flights in Paris in front of large crowds that were registered by the Aéro-Club of France as the first flights by a heavier-than-air vehicle flying and landing under its own power. The Wright Brothers' flight in the *Flyer* at Kitty Hawk in 1903 is generally seen as the first airplane flight. But Santos Dumont was also a true pioneer of aviation.

The legacy of Santos Dumont also shows that, for many in Brazil, even when one of their compatriots makes a significant contribution to science and technology, that achievement can be slighted by the superior public relations and marketing power of the Anglo-American world. This reinforces the mongrel dog complex (*complexo de vira lata*) that the playwright and journalist Nelson Rodrigues attributed to the Brazilian people, a feeling that they are seen by others as not good enough, not up to the standards of the so-called 'first world'. Brazilians are proud of their industrial might and their growing capacity in scientific research and technological development, and their contributions to academic fields such as pure mathematics, biochemistry, agronomy, environmental sciences, and tropical medicine. But they are also aware that they are isolated from the main centres of wealth and power in the world, residents of the southern hemisphere, and speakers of a language little known outside its borders and those of Portugal and her former colonies. Theirs is still a developing country, albeit a high middle-income one with an abundance of natural resources, including yet-unused arable land, vast reserves of water, and large deposits of offshore oil and gas. Whether Brazil can continue to innovate, to contribute to modernity, and whether it can be recognized for those contributions, are open questions.

Peaceful inclusion

Returning to the opening ceremony, another theme was Brazil's vocation for peace. Remember that the green tree projected on the floor of the Maracanã stadium was in the shape of a peace sign. Brazilian diplomats like to emphasize that the country pushed its borders westwards, well beyond the original limit set out in the Treaty of Tordesillas of 1494, largely through peaceful negotiations rather than military conquest (see Figure 2). Brazil has no major border disputes with any of its ten South American neighbours and its last participation in a war in the region ended in 1870.

One of its most revered heroes is a diplomat, the Baron of Rio Branco, who as Foreign Minister negotiated Brazil's last

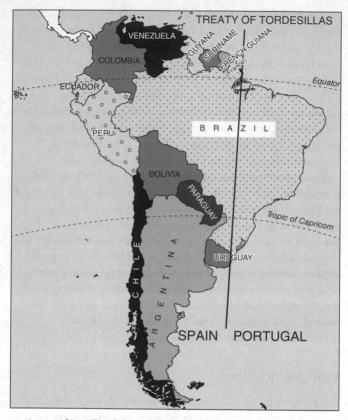

2. A map of Brazil and the rest of South America showing the line of the Treaty of Tordesillas, signed between Spain and Portugal in 1494.

remaining border conflicts in the early 20th century. More recently, Brazil could have built a nuclear weapon but chose not to. It does not want to be a superpower, and its diplomacy—until recently—emphasized multilateralism and the peaceful resolution of conflicts. It has honed a reputation as an important contributor to United Nations peacekeeping missions and headed the military component of MINUSTAH, the UN peacekeeping mission to Haiti, from 2004 to 2017. Peaceful inclusion, tolerance, and dialogue are said to be part of Brazilian identity and seen by some as characteristics of Brazil's history.

During the opening ceremony, the television presenter Regina Cassé said, 'Let's celebrate our differences', and the theme of the depiction of Brazilian history was 'Here in Brazil we mix'. Brazil is a country of racial and ethnic mixture, and its people tend not to adopt the hyphenated identities one can find in the United States. The Brazilian tendency towards dialogue and negotiation can also be seen in its confederal domestic politics, in which patient coalition building is necessary in a Congress with thirty different political parties.

Brazilian inclusivity begins with the indigenous population. There were an estimated 4 million indigenous people in the territory at the time that Pedro Álvares Cabral came ashore in what is now Brazil in 1500 to claim the territory for the Portuguese crown. The current indigenous population is below a million—less than half a per cent of the total population—but some 13 per cent of the national territory is land set aside for indigenous reserves. Most of these reserves are in the Amazon, making rainforest preservation and respect for indigenous rights connected issues. The 2010 census in Brazil identified 305 indigenous groups and 274 indigenous languages spoken in the country, most by very small numbers of people, since the national language, Portuguese, is well and truly national. In the opening ceremony, a group of dancers from Amazônia portrayed indigenous people on the floor of the Maracanã stadium, creating three huge *ocas* or lodges with brightly coloured elastic bands.

The ceremony also depicted the arrival of African slaves in chains. Brazil is home to the largest black population outside Africa, and Afro-Brazilian culture is at the heart of modern Brazil. Writing of the mixture of the indigenous, the African, and the European, the Brazilian anthropologist Gilberto Freyre claimed, in *The Masters and the Slaves* (1946; a translation of *Casa Grande e Senzala*,

9

1933) that every Brazilian has in his soul the mark of the indigenous or the African. But Brazil is more than the mixture of these three elements. The opening ceremony depicted the arrival of Syrians and Lebanese (called *turcos* in Brazil because they came from the lands of the Ottoman Empire), Japanese (Brazil has the largest population of people of Japanese descent outside of Japan), Italians, Germans, and Spaniards.

The ceremony also depicted capoeira, a hybrid martial art/dance that has been recognized by the United Nations Educational, Scientific, and Cultural Organization (UNESCO) as an intangible cultural heritage. It also depicted folkloric dances from different regions, such as Maracatu from Pernambuco, Aché from Salvador da Bahia, and bumba meu boi from Maranhão. Twelve major samba schools that perform in Rio's famous carnival were represented in the ceremony. Musical forms that were given space included bossa nova, Tropicália, funk, and hip-hop, as well as dances such as frevo, samba, and passinho. Brazilian supermodel Gisele Bündchen and Lea T., the first transgender woman to participate in an opening ceremony of the Olympic Games, were part of the performance. The head of the Brazilian Olympic Committee Carlos Arthur Nuzman emphasized the theme of inclusion when he said in his remarks, 'Let's stay together, despite our differences. Today the world is carioca [the name for a resident of Rio]. When the Olympic torch enters the stadium, it will bring a message to all Brazilians, a message of peace and unity.'

The narrative about Brazil's affinity for peace and inclusion has its critics inside and outside the country. As with all countries in the Americas, its history of the treatment of the indigenous population is replete with deception and violence. Similarly, few historians accept that slavery was more benign in Brazil than elsewhere. Brazil's last major war, fought with Argentina and Uruguay against Paraguay from 1864 to 1870, was a bloody affair that led to the annexation of Paraguayan territory and the decimation of its male population. Many major political transitions in Brazil, such as the abolition of slavery in 1888 and the creation of a republic in 1889, were made with relatively little inter-elite conflict. However, there are many examples in Brazil's history of violent suppression of resistance from below. To give a recent example, the preparation for the Olympic Games in Rio involved the forcible relocation of several thousand families whose homes were in the way of development projects. And despite its peaceful foreign policy, contemporary Brazil is a violent society, with a murder rate almost five times the world average. In 2018 it recorded 57,358 killings, the largest number of any country in the world that year. The police were responsible for about 11 per cent of those killings. Most of the victims of all types of killing were young non-white males. This leads to the question of whether Brazil can credibly promote peace abroad when its own society is racked by violence.

Informality

The fourth theme dealt with by the Olympic opening ceremony in Rio in 2016 was the distinctive Brazilian way of getting things done. One of the directors of the ceremony, the film-maker Fernando Meirelles, whose budget had been cut, said that the show had been delivered through *gambiarra*, or a kind of homemade improvisation. Brazilians are proud of their ability to improvise, to adjust to circumstances, and to make do without the resources and infrastructure of richer countries. They live in a society where trust in public institutions is low. One way to overcome this lack of trust is to rely on extended family relationships and, if dealing outside the family, to build direct personal relationships with interlocutors in which informal understandings can be as important as formal procedures.

One of Brazil's folkloric characters, the *malandro* or artful dodger, is someone who uses a *jeito*, or dodge, to get around cumbersome rules. Historically, Brazilians across the class spectrum have found *gambiarra*, *jeito*, or *jeitinho* (little dodge) necessary to solve problems, because the law has been so formal, so cumbersome, and so out of touch with social realities that it makes many simple things impossible. In the face of these obstacles, *malandragem*, the art of the *malandro*, has been celebrated as a way of dealing with harsh realities.

Brazilians have a right to be proud of this creativity, spontaneity, and assertiveness. These traits have stood them in good stead when faced with scarcity and social problems. But *malandragem* has a dark side. It can move from constructive, collective problem-solving of a positive nature into collusion, anti-social attitudes, and criminality. This is a challenge for the construction and maintenance of a democratic rule of law. Brazil's major anti-corruption investigation, called Carwash (*Lava Jato*) because it began as an inquiry into money laundering in an office above a carwash in Brasília, started in March of 2014. It has uncovered widespread and systematic political corruption in the country, including kickbacks for government contracts, illegal campaign finance, and bribes to the executives of state-owned firms and elected officials. This has led to unprecedented levels of distrust of government on the part of the Brazilian electorate. During the opening ceremony of the Olympics, when the head of the Brazilian Olympic Committee Carlos Arthur Nuzman acknowledged the efforts of the three levels of government, federal, state and municipal, to make the games a reality, many in the audience booed.

On 5 October 2017 the Carwash investigation came right into the heart of the Brazilian Olympic Committee. The Federal Police arrested Carlos Arthur Nuzman on the suspicion that in 2009 he had bribed a member of the International Olympic Committee to vote for Rio as the site of the 2016 games. The Carwash investigation also led to charges being brought in the Supreme Court against a sitting president, Michel Temer, in 2017, as well as the appeals court conviction and imprisonment of a former president, Luiz Inácio 'Lula' da Silva in 2018, an event that took the most popular candidate out of the presidential campaign of that year. The governor of Rio at the time of the 2016 Olympic Games, Sérgio Cabral, was convicted in a series of trials from 2017 to 2020 on charges of bribe-taking and money laundering. First arrested about three months after the opening ceremony of the Olympic Games, he was sentenced to a cumulative total of 280 years in prison. Whether Brazil can move from these scandals into a new equilibrium in which political corruption is no longer endemic is an important question.

How did Brazil become Brazil?

Since the mid-1980s, when its twenty-one-year military dictatorship came to an end, Brazil has improved as a country. It promulgated its most democratic constitution ever in 1988. Progress can be seen in statistics such as those about infant mortality, life expectancy, literacy, nutrition, health, and education levels. Brazil has become more socially inclusive, and its democratic political institutions have endured. Looking farther back over the last 100 years, it is clear that globally, Brazil has become a more important country. In the early 20th century it was a relative backwater and not one of the top ten economies in the world. In the first part of the 21st century it is, with its agricultural, mineral, and even some manufactured exports, reaching markets worldwide. But as the opening ceremony of the Rio Olympics showed, Brazil's sources of national pride are complicated and sometimes ambiguous and contradictory. Behind the undeniable achievements are anxieties and doubts.

The national themes outlined here are the result of more than 500 years of history. They were shaped in the period when Brazil was still a Portuguese colony, then an independent empire, and later still a republic. But they came to maturity relatively late, only in the last 100 years. This book will explore Brazil's national trajectory by looking at two important historical periods and three important contemporary issues. The two periods are the one dominated by President Getúlio Vargas (1930–45 and 1951–4), when Brazil's national state was consolidated and the national territory effectively integrated, and the military dictatorship (1964–85), when twin projects of conservative modernization of the economy and political reshaping and repression were pursued. The three contemporary issues concern the hard choices involved in the management of the economy; debates about citizenship, representation, and the quality of democracy; and the role of Brazil in the multipolar world. But before embarking on that journey, it is important to describe some elements of Brazilian history before the revolution that brought Getúlio Vargas, the leading political figure of Brazil's 20th century, to power.

Chapter 2
From colony to empire to republic

It is only in the 20th century that Brazil could be said to have had all three essential components of a modern nation-state: a clearly defined national territory, a state with the capacity to administer that territory, and a people with a shared identity. Compared to ancient states such as China or India, or European states such as Portugal and France, Brazil is a relatively recent creation. For more than three centuries it was a colony of Portugal, and for the first sixty-seven years of its independent history it was a monarchy and an empire rather than a republic. This unusual set of circumstances gives Brazil a unique path to statehood and nationhood in the Americas, one that will be the focus of this chapter.

Several elements of Brazil's history before the last century stand out. First, it began as a remote and relatively unimportant outpost of a seaborne empire, the Portuguese, in which the main object of interest was the East, and especially Goa in India. Second, the Portuguese empire was based on commerce and diplomacy more than a strong army and military occupation. Third, unlike the Spanish Empire in the New World, Brazil did not fragment into a number of different countries after independence. Instead, it retained and expanded its territorial reach over time. That did not mean, however, that it was a strongly unified whole. The vast territory was only loosely held together, and for parts of its colonial history was governed as two separate regions. (This is why it was often referred to as the Brazils, rather than Brazil.) Finally, for much of its history it was regarded by many outside observers as inferior to Europe because of its racial mixture and reliance on slavery. Charles Darwin, for example, was appalled by the submissiveness of a black slave whom he met near Rio in 1832 and condemned the man's degradation in *The Voyage of the Beagle*, his travel memoir published in 1839. Brazil's racial mixture was also considered to be a severe disadvantage by many Europeans and North Americans influenced by the pseudo-scientific racism of the 19th century, and it was only in the 20th century that this alleged 'handicap' became, in the eyes of many, an asset.

The indigenous

Aikanã. Banawá. Inranxe. Kaapor. Kanindé. Munduruku. Tupinambá. Xavante. Yanomami. These are some of the 305 indigenous groups in Brazil, descendants of the original inhabitants of South America. Some of these indigenous groups straddle national borders and their members have relatives in neighbouring countries such as Bolivia, Paraguay, Peru, Colombia, Venezuela, Suriname, and Guyana. The indigenous peoples of the Americas are thought to have walked across the Bering Strait or travelled by boat from Asia more than 20,000 years ago.

Unlike the Aztecs in Mexico and the Inca in Peru, the indigenous of Brazil encountered by the Europeans were not part of a large empire or an urban civilization. (Although evidence of large settlements in the Amazon has been uncovered by archaeologists.) Instead, they were nomadic hunter-gatherers. The French missionary Jean de Léry, who arrived in what is now Rio de Janeiro in 1557 and stayed for ten months, left a remarkable record of the indigenous Tupis whom he encountered during his visit. The Tupis planted and harvested cassava (manioc), believing that nature would provide for their children as it provided for them. Tupi society seemed to lack the destructive dynamism and insecure acquisitiveness of post-feudal Europe. It is said that the philosopher Jean-Jacques Rousseau drew on de Léry's memoir for his theorizing about the state of nature and the corrupting influence of modern society. The Portuguese colonists wanted to exploit Indian labour, while missionaries sought to convert the Indians to Christianity. The Jesuits were responsible for Indian welfare in Brazil until they were expelled from the colony in the 1760s. Disease decimated the ranks of the indigenous, and many tribes moved inland to escape Portuguese exploitation.

The indigenous presence in contemporary Brazil is not as strong as it is in other Latin American countries such as Mexico or Peru. Few of Brazil's national symbols contain indigenous leitmotifs such as the Aztec eagle grasping a snake on the Mexican flag. However, many names for animals, plants, and places in Brazilian Portuguese come from indigenous languages. Examples of the first are toucan, tapir, jacaré (alligator), and jaguar; caju (cashew) is an example of the second, and Guanabara, the name for the bay in Rio de Janeiro, as well as the states of Amapá and Tocantins, of the third. While the indigenous have suffered greatly in Brazil, there has been a resurgence of indigenous activism, as well as a revalorization of their contributions to the nation in recent decades. For example, there are now some 60,000 indigenous students in Brazilian universities, in a total university student population of 8.29 million, making them 0.7 per cent of the total, close to their percentage of the total population.

The Portuguese

The Portuguese reached what is now Brazil because it was they, of all the European peoples, who first journeyed beyond their borders in an attempt to proselytize, trade with, and sometimes subjugate people in South America, Africa, and Asia. Portugal, a country with a population of at most a million and a quarter in the mid-16th century, which at that time possessed the biggest and most powerful high seas fleet in Europe, became rich from trade with the Indies.

The Spanish call their creation of an empire in the Americas the 'conquista', the conquest. The Portuguese call their empire the 'descobrimentos', the discoveries, and that difference says something about the nature of colonialism carried out by the two countries. Portugal created what the historian Charles Boxer called a seaborne empire. In its colonies Portugal often did not control much territory inland, but established forts along the coast that allowed it to control trade. The Portuguese knew that theirs was a small nation and that they had to rely more on guile than strength. Diplomacy and negotiation were important elements of their expansion.

In 1500 Pedro Álvares Cabral, a nobleman working for the Portuguese crown, reached the coast of what is now Brazil. Cabral, then about 32 or 33 years old, commanded a fleet of thirteen ships and 1,200 men. On 22 April the fleet sighted land and anchored near what Cabral called 'Monte Pascoal' (since it was Easter week). On 23 April Cabral ordered Nicolau Coelho to go ashore and make contact with the indigenous people (Tupiniquins) whom they could see on the shore. Coelho went ashore with some gifts, and then they sailed north to a natural harbour which Cabral called Porto Seguro (Safe Port), now a town on the coast of the state of Bahia. There, the Portuguese built a massive wooden cross and an altar where they held mass on 1 May. Cabral believed the land to be an island and christened it the Ilha de Vera Cruz—the Island of the True Cross. He then sent a supply ship back to Portugal to tell the king about what he had found. This ship contained a detailed letter from Pero Vaz de Caminha, one of Cabral's crew members, that described the land and people they had visited. Some historians have called this letter Brazil's 'birth certificate'.

Cabral's arrival in Brazil looks today like a very significant event for the Portuguese Empire, but at the time it was not seen—by the Portuguese at least—as very important. Cabral was on his way to India. Unlike Cortés's arrival in Mexico in 1519 or Pizarro's conquest of Peru in 1533, Cabral's visit to Brazil did not uncover any evidence of great wealth. For most of the 16th century Brazil remained a backwater, a station for the provisioning of Portuguese ships on their way to India. The two most important products shipped from Brazil to Portugal were pau brasil and sugar, which was first planted in Madeira and Cape Verde and then in Pernambuco, in the north-east, and São Vicente, in what is now the state of São Paulo, near Santos. Almost everything that Brazil needed was shipped from Portugal or—in the case of slaves—from Africa. But the real prize for the Portuguese was the Indian Ocean trade in spices, and the jewel in the Portuguese crown was 'golden Goa'.

Both the Spanish and the Portuguese in the 16th century were obsessed with race, 'purity of blood', and so-called 'contaminated races'. They had overturned Moorish rule in the Iberian peninsula in the Reconquista and Spain expelled practising Jews in 1492 as part of the Inquisition. Tens of thousands of Spanish Jews then went to Portugal. In 1497 King Manuel of Portugal decreed that all Jews had to convert to Christianity or leave the country. This led to the conversion, genuine or otherwise, of many Jewish people to Catholicism. The Portuguese Inquisition was established in 1536 and eventually expanded its reach within the Portuguese Empire, largely targeting so-called New Christians (converts from Judaism). The New Christians often took non-noble names such as Azevedo, Figueiredo, Oliveira, and Pereira. As a result of this repression, thousands of Jews fled Portugal and went to Amsterdam, London, and other cities, as well as the New World. The first synagogue in the Americas was established in Recife in 1636 when the Dutch were ruling Pernambuco. After the Dutch were expelled from the area in 1654, some from this community went to the Caribbean and later New York City, then called New Amsterdam.

Africans

Because disease sickened and killed so many of the indigenous, and the Portuguese sought labour for their plantations, a transition from indigenous to African slavery took place in Brazil in the second half of the 16th century. An estimated 4 million Africans (perhaps as much as 40 per cent of the entire Atlantic slave trade) were imported into Brazil in the three centuries between 1550 and 1850. The slaves came from the Egyptian Sudan, the coast of the Gulf of Guinea, the Congo, Angola, Mozambique, and elsewhere on the African continent. Ethnic groups among the enslaved included the Bakongo, Mbundu, Benguela, and Ovambo in Angola and the Yoruba, Ewe, Minas, Hausa, Nupe, and Borno in west Africa. The two largest ports receiving slaves in the trade to Brazil were Salvador and Rio de Janeiro.

African contributions to Brazil's economy, culture, and society were immense (see Figure 3). At the beginning of the 19th century, Brazil had the largest slave population in the world—roughly 50 per cent of its population of 3 million people. Brazilian slave importation was greater than that for all of Spanish America, and ten times that of North America. (The Brazilian slave population did not reproduce itself as its North American counterpart did due to disease and overwork.) At the end of the colonial period in the early 19th century, Afro-Brazilians made up a majority of the population in the four largest provinces—75 per cent in Minas Gerais, 68 per cent in Pernambuco, 79 per cent in Bahia, and 64 per cent in Rio de Janeiro. Only in São Paulo were whites in the majority (56 per cent of the total). Unlike in the southern United States, a large percentage of the non-white population—roughly 42 per cent at the end of the colonial period—were free. This was in part because manumission was easier than it was in the United States. Slave revolts were not uncommon: there were eight between 1807 and 1844. Furthermore, hundreds of communities of escaped

3.   An 1839 print of a painting by the French artist Jean-Baptiste Debret showing a family in Rio with its slaves.

slaves, called *quilombos*, were created when Brazil was a Portuguese colony. The largest and most famous of these was Palmares, established in what is now Alagoas at the end of the 16th century. It was said to have had 20,000 residents and resisted several Portuguese and Dutch attempts to destroy it. Palmares was finally wiped out by the Portuguese in 1694 and its leader Zumbi, a descendant of warriors from Angola, was killed the following year.

The gold rush

For more than 300 years, Brazil was a colony of Portugal, a declining power in western Europe. Its economy was dominated by the labour-intensive production of sugar and later coffee, and supplemented by cotton, tobacco, meat, and other agricultural products. Luxury items such as wine and intellectual products such as books were imported from Europe. Unlike Spain, Portugal did not permit the establishment of universities in its colonies, nor did it permit printing presses. However, at the end of the 17th century, the colony underwent an important change.

In 1695 *bandeirantes* or adventurers from São Paulo discovered gold and later precious stones in what is now the state of Minas Gerais (General Mines). The subsequent gold rush transformed the country, strengthened the colonial state, and altered the relations between the metropole and the colony. Some 600,000 Portuguese from continental Portugal and the Atlantic islands came to Brazil between 1700 and 1760. Miners and their slaves poured into the province from other parts of Brazil. The Portuguese crown strengthened its presence in Minas Gerais in order to collect its *quinto*, a 20 per cent tax on all mined gold, and *capitação*, a head tax on all miners and slaves over the age of 12. Tribunals with appointed judges were established to collect the taxes. Portugal sent two companies of army soldiers to Minas Gerais in 1719.

Gold mining peaked in the first half of the 18th century, but Minas Gerais remained a heavily populated and important province in colonial and post-colonial times. It was in this province that a pro-independence conspiracy involving landowners, clerics, intellectuals, and members of the military was uncovered by the Portuguese in 1789, the year of the French revolution. The conspirators were charged with *lèse-majesté*, an offence against the sovereign. One of them, Joaquim José da Silva Xavier, a dentist known as Tiradentes (toothpuller), was executed on 21 April 1792. The republican government that came to power in 1889 made the day of his death a national holiday, turning him into a hero of Brazilian nationalism.

The colonial state had a dual character. It was capable and relatively sophisticated in the cities, most of which were on the coast, but in the vast interior it was notable for its absence. There, large landowners exercised many of the powers of the state and did so personally, arbitrarily, and often despotically. The historian Sérgio Buarque de Holanda called this Brazilian figure the *homem cordial*, the cordial man. Despite the warm overtones of the phrase, Buarque de Holanda's cordial man was an enemy of an egalitarian public sphere. Trust in public institutions in colonial Brazil was low. The gap between the formal intentions of the colonial state, based in Lisbon, and the implementation of policy in distant Brazil, was great. Connection to a powerful landed family was an important element of survival for the rural poor. Historians have called this state patrimonial, meaning that it allowed for the conflation of private and public power in the hands of landed families. This pattern endured into independence. In the 19th century, according to the literary theorist Roberto Schwarz, Brazil was marked by a mismatch between the professed liberal ideals of its elites and the reality that its economy was based on slavery. Schwarz called this mismatch ideas out of place.

The court comes to Rio

In 1807 the Napoleonic Wars made a strong impact on Portugal, and consequently Brazil. French troops crossed the border between Spain and Portugal and marched towards Lisbon. The Portuguese monarchy and its court, numbering between 10,000 and 15,000 people, boarded Portuguese ships and crossed the Atlantic, protected by a fleet of the British Navy. They arrived in Rio de Janeiro in April 1808, bringing with them a printing press, the royal treasury, and libraries that would establish the foundation for the National Library.

During this period Dom João VI of the Braganza royal family made many concessions to the British in return for the preservation of his dynasty. He ended the monopoly with Portugal and opened some Brazilian ports, legalizing trade with Great Britain and giving a strong commercial advantage to British merchants. An 1810 treaty limited tariffs on British exports to Brazil at 15 per cent. When Dom João VI reluctantly returned to

Portugal he left his son, Dom Pedro I, on the throne in Brazil, effectively splitting the Portuguese monarchy in two.

It was Dom Pedro I who, in 1822, declared Brazilian independence. This monarchical version of independence set Brazil apart from its Spanish American neighbours, many of whom had fought bloody wars against the Spanish crown and had established republics. Brazilian royalists credited the monarchy with Brazil's relative stability in the 19th century. The central state suppressed secessionist revolts and slave uprisings, and the country did not fragment. Dom Pedro I's son Dom Pedro II ruled from 1831 to 1889. Chile on the west coast and Brazil on the east coast were the two most capable states in 19th-century South America, consolidating and expanding their territory through the power of their navies and armies and, in Brazil's case, through the skill of its diplomats.

The alliance between Portugal and Britain, the naval superpower of the 19th century, was seen as essential for the Portuguese because of the vulnerability of their far-flung seaborne empire. Newly independent Brazil inherited this military and economic dependence on the British through the Braganza royal family. The British forced the Brazilians to sign a treaty in 1826 that formally eliminated the slave trade. The Brazilians used a revealing expression for their approach to the suppression of the slave trade, something that they had no capacity or interest in enforcing—*para o ingles ver* ('for the English to see'). Their commitment was more formal than real. There were many clandestine importations of slaves in the two decades that followed the signing of the treaty. An example was the covert landings at the Porto de Galinhas in Pernambuco, the Chicken Port ('chicken' was a euphemism for slaves). Landowners went to great lengths to disguise the illegal importation of slaves during this period, falsifying dates of entry and using other forms of chicanery to elude law enforcement, while some slaves who arrived in Brazil though the illegal trade went to court to demand their freedom, with mixed results. *Para o ingles ver* has remained a common expression in Brazil to indicate keeping up appearances, outwardly adhering to formal rules of some kind, while informally behaving in a very different manner. The gap between formal and informal rules remains an important way to understand Brazilian politics, and the common phrase 'the law did not stick' (*a lei não pegou*) indicates that not all aspects of formal legality are necessarily applied, or at least not applied consistently, in the country.

It was only in 1850 and 1851 that Brazil effectively ended the slave trade. A combination of domestic and international factors led the Brazilian government to finally act. Two decades later the government began to abolish slavery itself in a piecemeal and conservative fashion. The Law of the Free Womb, passed in 1871, granted freedom to all people born as slaves when they turned 21. The provinces of Ceará and Amazonas abolished slavery in 1884. An 1885 law freed slaves 60 and older. And the 1888 Golden Law liberated the remaining 600,000 slaves. Landowners' demands for compensation for the loss of their slaves were ignored, but so were calls for the distribution of land to the newly freed population. A factor that made abolition politically manageable was the realization that Europeans could be persuaded to come to work in the country and replace slaves.

War

The Brazilian Foreign Ministry congratulates itself for Brazil's record of peaceful coexistence with its ten South American neighbours. However, Brazil did engage in a major war in the 19th century, one that led to the deaths of perhaps more than 300,000. This was the war against Paraguay, fought in alliance with Argentina and Uruguay, from 1864 to 1870. After the end of the war, Brazilian troops did not leave Asunción, Paraguay's capital, until 1876.

The Brazilian view of the war is that it was brought about by the truculence of the Paraguayan dictator Francisco Solano López, who invaded both Argentine and Brazilian territory. The Paraguayan perspective sees its three neighbours as imperialistic aggressors who took advantage of a smaller nation that stood up for its rights. Although it faced much larger countries, at the beginning of the war, the Paraguayan army was larger than the Argentine, Uruguayan, and Brazilian forces put together. The early course of the war showed Brazil's lack of preparedness for large-scale military conflict, but in time the strength of the superior force of the three allies proved decisive. Brazilian atrocities, including the sacking of Asunción in 1869, are still remembered in Paraguay and Brazilian troops killed Solano López in the last and decisive battle of the war at Cerro Corá.

Brazil's participation in the Paraguay War strengthened the armed forces within the state and weakened the monarchy. Within the army a group of positivist officers, inspired by the French philosopher August Comte and his views of the possibility of a rationalist and incremental improvement of society, were influential. These officers were a driving force in the abolition of slavery, the toppling of the monarchy a year later in 1889, and the proclamation of a republic with a new coat of arms and a new flag, inscribed with the Comtean motto 'order and progress'. The army was also used to suppress potential revolts inside the country, as when it destroyed a religious community and killed most of the men in Canudos, in the interior of the north-east of Brazil, in 1897, an event memorably described by the journalist Euclides da Cunha in his book *Rebellion in the Backlands* (*Os Sertões*) (Figure 4).

The first republic

The republic was born of the first—but not the last—military coup in Brazil's history. On 15 November 1889 a group of army officers and their civilian supporters deposed Emperor Dom Pedro II. The

4. The body of Antônio Conselheiro, leader of the settlement in Canudos, after he died in the siege by the Brazilian army.

leaders of the new government allowed the emperor and his family to go into exile. Dom Pedro II died two years later in Paris. In 1920 a republican government allowed his remains to be repatriated to Brazil, as Brazil finally reconciled its monarchical past with its republican present.

The republic brought about a number of changes. Internationally, Brazil abandoned its traditional attachment to Europe. It realigned its foreign policy to move closer to the United States, the biggest buyer of its main export, coffee. And it also moved closer to its neighbours to the south, Argentina and Uruguay. The Baron of Rio Branco, the patron saint of Brazilian diplomacy and foreign minister from 1902 to 1912, supervised this important transition in Brazilian foreign policy and also helped to resolve Brazil's disputes with several of the countries along its 16,885-kilometre land border, the third longest in the world after Russia's and China's. By 1912 it could be said that Brazil's territorial existence was, after more than 400 years, fully resolved. Rio Branco also embodied a certain idea of Brazil and its role in the world that until recently was cherished in Brazil's Foreign Ministry:

cultivated, erudite, devoted to multilateralism, international law, peaceful coexistence, and compromise based on negotiation.

Domestically, Brazil was ruled by military presidents for the first five years of the republic. This was a tumultuous period that saw many conflicts, including a rebellion by the Brazilian navy in 1893–4 that was put down by the government of President Floriano Peixoto with the help of five US warships. This revolt was memorably portrayed by Lima Barreto in his novel *The Sad End of Policarpo Quaresma*, published in 1915. The political system later evolved into a civilian regime largely dominated by great landowners.

It was during the republic that immigration to Brazil accelerated. Immigrants came from Italy, Spain, Germany, and Portugal, as well as the Ottoman Empire, Japan, and (later) eastern Europe. The total number of immigrants between 1890 and 1930 is estimated at 3,800,000, or 22 per cent of the 17 million Brazilians counted in the 1900 census. Immigrants were welcomed by the Brazilian government, which often paid the costs of passage. They were viewed both as a source of labour (especially in coffee in São Paulo but also in small farms in the south) and a means of 'whitening' and thereby supposedly improving the population.

Foreign views of Brazil were often infused with negativity that derived from pseudo-scientific racism. For example, in a book published by British travellers Ulick Ralph Burke and Robert Staples Jr in 1886, just three years before the establishment of the republic, they wrote, 'The province of São Paulo has great natural advantages and if 100,000 Anglo-Saxon emigrants were turned into it they could make a fine country of it; but the Brazilians are incompetent, and can or will do nothing.' The central government during the republic was weak. Until 1889 it was the dynastic figure of the emperor who embodied national unity. Regional movements contested the central government, so that Brazil still faced many of the challenges of creating a national political order that had already been met by its Spanish American neighbours—particularly Argentina, Chile, and Uruguay—a generation before.

Brazil and the 20th century

At the dawn of the 20th century, Brazil was seen by many contemporaries (both foreign and Brazilian) as lacking many of the constitutive elements of a modern nation-state. Its racially mixed population doomed it, in this popular view, to second-class status among the community of nations. Its vast territory was loosely held together by a weak central government and political parties that were little more than regional conglomerations of landowning families. The vast majority of the population worked in agriculture and standards of literacy and health were low. There were elections, but the franchise was tiny. Many Brazilian intellectuals were pessimistic about the chances of their country achieving economic development and some degree of democratization of social and political life. The structures of economic dependence forged by centuries of colonial and neocolonial exploitation were seen as too strong, and social hierarchies and patterns of privilege and exclusion too entrenched.

However, in the 20th century, change did occur. Within a few decades, Brazil had all three essential components of a modern nation-state: a clearly defined national territory, a state with the capacity to administer that territory, and a people with a shared identity. That achievement was symbolized by an uprising known as the revolution of 1930. It is to that event that we now turn.

Chapter 3
The Vargas era and its legacy

Politics during most of the first republic (1889–1930) could best be described as a set of negotiations between regional elites. In this decentralized system, the leaders of the state party machines were the power brokers, which is why 'the politics of the governors' is often used to describe it. The two most important states, São Paulo and Minas Gerais, alternated control of the presidency in an arrangement dubbed coffee and milk, reflecting the fact that coffee was the most important crop in the first state, and the dairy industry paramount in the second. In many states, party machines controlled the government with a mixture of electoral fraud and intimidation. The idea that the government would address social concerns of workers was considered anathema by many in power. One of the presidents of the first republic, Washington Luís (1926–30), was said to have called the social question a matter for the police.

However, the cosy accommodations between elites of the first republic were threatened in the early 20th century by a series of events with global repercussions. The First World War (1914–18), a gruesome conflict involving the mass slaughter of trench warfare, artillery bombardments, and chemical weapons, tarnished the achievements of European civilization and led intellectuals and artists in Brazil and elsewhere to question the superiority of European modes of thought. The February and October revolutions of 1917 destroyed the Russian monarchy and aristocracy and brought the Bolsheviks to power. The Bolshevik idea of workers' control through soviets was seized on by working-class militants and aspiring revolutionaries outside Russia, including Latin America, and the Brazilian Communist Party was founded in 1922.

Furthermore, the Brazilian military was shaken by a movement of young lieutenants who wanted a strong central state that could educate the population, promote industrialization, and improve electoral transparency. A number of revolts inside the armed forces carried out by officers who espoused these principles rocked Brazil in the 1920s. At the end of the decade, the stock market crash on Wall Street in 1929 led to a fall in the price of commodities, including Brazil's chief export, coffee, which in turn generated political instability.

Brazil's 1930 revolution—hardly a social revolution along the lines of Mexico in 1910 or Russia in 1917—represented the culmination of this ferment of the 1910s and 1920s. Shaped by international developments and triggered by a conflict over the succession to the presidency, the revolution led to the formation of a new kind of state in Brazil and a new set of state–citizen relations. The political figure who dominated the period after the revolution was Getúlio Vargas, an astute, taciturn landowner and former army officer from Rio Grande do Sul. Vargas had a political career as a district attorney, state legislator, leader of the Rio Grande do Sul caucus in the lower house of the National Congress, minister of finance for President Washington Luís, and governor of Rio Grande do Sul. He ran for president under the Liberal Alliance in 1930, and when he was declared the loser of the election, conspired with allies in Minas Gerais and Paraíba to depose the elected government and become president, winning over parts of the military in the process.

After seizing power, Vargas served as president for fifteen years, first as head of the provisional government, then as an indirectly elected president, and finally as a dictator. Removed from power in 1945, he returned in a new guise as a developmentalist president elected in 1950. This chapter will explore how the various currents of the Vargas era came together to transform the Brazilian economy, polity, and society.

The 1930 revolution

Vargas had developed his political skills in the state of Rio Grande do Sul, where open warfare between the Republican Party and the Federalist Party (later the Liberator Party) occurred between 1893 and 1895 and again in 1923. Getúlio's father General Manuel do Nascimento Vargas was a veteran of the Paraguay War and a member of the Republican Party in São Borja, in the west of the state near the border with Argentina. When Vargas became president (as the position was then called) of Rio Grande do Sul in 1928, he succeeded his patron Antônio Augusto Borges de Medeiros, who had been president of the state for thirty years.

The 1930 revolution weakened traditional elites in the country, particularly those connected to coffee. It solidified a new pact between the Catholic Church and the state, symbolized by the unveiling of the statue of Christ the Redeemer in Rio de Janeiro in October 1931, in which Vargas and his ministers took part, and a decree in the same year permitting the teaching of religion in state schools. It also centralized power in the national state. All governors except the newly elected governor of Minas Gerais were replaced by *interventores*, hand-picked representatives of the central government. But it was perhaps with regard to labour that the new government was most innovative.

In November 1930, only a few days after Vargas became president, the government created a new Ministry of Labour, Industry, and Commerce. The ministry reversed the labour policies of the first republic, which had basically regarded labour organizations as criminal conspiracies, and began to formally recognize and register trade unions. In March 1931 new regulations for workers' and employers' associations were promulgated. The government used its power to exclude from registration those unions led by the Communist Party and radical leaders such as the anarchists. In this way it created a corporatist system of labour representation in which state recognition and support went hand in hand with state control and ideological vetting. The government also prevented the creation of a nationwide trade union federation. Shop floor organization and grass-roots mobilization tended to be weak in Brazil's labour relations system.

The Vargas regime also created a network of labour courts that still exist today (although the Ministry of Labour was abolished in 2019). The idea behind the creation of the courts was that the state needed to adjudicate labour disputes both to preserve domestic harmony and to compensate for the weakness of labour in conflicts and collective bargaining. The labour court system, whose pinnacle is the Superior Labour Court, adjudicates cases involving individual workers bringing claims against their employers as well as trade unions seeking new and improved collective contracts.

The labour court system divides opinion in Brazil. Some, especially economic liberals, view it as part of an unacceptable holdover from the past, one that elevates the cost and uncertainty of doing business in Brazil. Others view it as a system that gives workers some chance of redress and defence of their rights in an order that is otherwise often stacked against them. Still others view the labour courts critically from the left, as a set of institutions that oppresses workers and enshrines the interests of employers and the state.

Art, culture, and ideas

The 1930 revolution brought into the heart of the state many of the ideas, previously thought of as vanguardist, developed in the

1920s and the 1930s. Modernism, a literary and artistic movement that came to prominence during Modern Art Week from 11 to 18 February in 1922 in São Paulo, went mainstream in the Vargas regime. The Ministry of Education and Health, created in November 1930, was one ministry that promoted modernism. The headquarters of the ministry in Rio de Janeiro, completed in 1943, was designed by modernist architects including Lúcio Costa and Oscar Niemeyer, later famous for their work designing Brasília. The building contained a mural by Cândido Portinari, known for his paintings of Brazilian workers, including the coffee picker (*O Lavrador de Café*) painted in 1934.

Modern Art Week was, in part, a reaction to the horrors of the First World War and an extension and reinterpretation of the proto-nationalist movements in Brazil in the 19th century, including romanticism. Modernist writers and artists sought inspiration not in European forms and conventions but in Brazilian images, ideas, and themes, such as nature, the indigenous, and the life of people in the interior of the country. Oswald de Andrade's *Anthropophagic Manifesto* of 1928, for example, seized on the ritualized cannibalism of some Brazilian indigenous tribes as a metaphor for Brazilians' approach to the world. Instead of simply imitating the culture of the rich countries, Brazilians could ingest the culture of the 'other', absorbing it and making it their own, producing something that was more authentically national than the art that had been produced before.

In literature, Oswald de Andrade's friend Mário de Andrade published a picaresque novel called *Macunaíma* in 1928. *Macunaíma* parodies indigenous folk tales to satirize the urban Brazil of the 1920s. The painter Tarsila do Amaral experimented with different styles and created, among other paintings, *Abaporu* (1928), inspired by indigenous understandings of the world and credited with stimulating the anthropophagic movement in the arts in Brazil. Modernists tried to convince their various audiences that modernism was Brazil and Brazil was modernism. By building a coalition of state bureaucrats, critics, and diplomats posted abroad, the modernists were able to associate their art and their ideas with the image of the country. The nationalist and authoritarian sentiments of most modernists also converged comfortably with the objectives of the Vargas regime.

The centralizing regime and resistance

In the 1930s, the Vargas regime built up the federal bureaucracy and shaped an increasingly capable central state with administrative control over the national territory. It also began to promote national identity using the power of the new medium of the time, radio, as well as theatre, cinema, conferences, expositions, concerts, civic and cultural events, texts, and images. This identity was largely secular and revolved around the Portuguese language, the national project of economic development, shared pastimes such as football (soccer) and samba, and the figure of Vargas. If Argentina, Chile, and Uruguay were the most advanced South American states at this time, Brazil made considerable progress after 1930. Brazil had little to fear from its neighbours. The threats that drove state builders in Brazil were largely internal. The Administrative Department of the Public Service, DASP (Departamento Administrativo do Serviço Público) was created in 1937. It promulgated a statute of federal civil servants (1939), promoted 'scientific' methods of public administration, and trained civil servants, enhancing the state's administrative capabilities.

The strengthening of the central state's capacity was not welcomed by everyone. In 1932 the state of São Paulo engaged in a revolt against the federal government. The revolt, carried out in the name of constitutionalism, was a reaction by the São Paulo coffee planters to the Vargas government's marginalization of their interests. The Vargas government's reaction included the bombing of the civilian population of São Paulo. After the deaths of more than 2,000 combatants in three months of fighting, São Paulo acceded to the reimposition of federal control. The memory of this uprising shaped the Vargas regime. President Getúlio Vargas said to the Congressman Valdemar Ferreira in 1937 that his focus was on the maintenance of order because he did not want what occurred in 1932 in the Paulista Revolution to happen again.

The federal government claimed executive and legislative authority after the revolt. The army was made more powerful. The state militias were subordinated to the army. Vargas was particularly worried about the Força Pública of São Paulo. Critics thought that it was excessively militarized. The 1934 Constitution and Law 192 of 1936 addressed this issue by making the state police the reservists of the armed forces. This principle was preserved in the 1937 Constitution. Getúlio Vargas said in Petropolis in 1937, 'The Armed Forces will never permit other flags to wave higher than ours.' In the same year, on 27 November, Vargas organized a ceremony in Rio in which the twenty state flags were burned.

In 1934 the National Liberatory Alliance, an anti-fascist popular front largely dominated by the Brazilian Communist Party (Partido Comunista Brasileiro, or PCB), promulgated a leftist programme of nationalization of industries and agrarian reform. The Vargas government reacted by passing a National Security Law in 1935 that outlawed the alliance. The Communist Party then organized a revolt known as the Intentona in November 1935. The uprising, which took place inside the armed forces and amongst civilians, occurred in the north-eastern cities of Natal and Recife as well as Rio de Janeiro. It led to the deaths of at least twenty-two legalist troops and afterwards the Vargas regime violently repressed the Brazilian Communist Party. In September 1936 it also created a National Security Tribunal to try alleged Communists and others viewed by the authorities as subversive threats to the political order. This special court judged hundreds of cases before it was abolished in 1945.

In the 1930s a Brazilian fascist movement, the Integralists, arose. Inspired by Italian fascism, the Brazilian Integralist Action was founded in 1932, led by the writer and journalist Plínio Salgado, and claimed to have between 600,000 and 1 million members at its peak in 1936. In their marches, the integralists wore green shirts, black ties, and black or white trousers. Using the Greek letter sigma rather than a swastika as their symbol, they made a salute similar to the Nazi one, and their slogan '*anauê*' was supposed to be a Tupi word that meant 'you are my brother'. Since the Vargas regime's authoritarian, nationalist, and anti-Communist outlook occupied most of the space claimed by the fascists, the Integralists' popular support was limited, and they were repressed after their attempted coup in 1938.

The Black Brazilian Front or Frente Negra Brasileira was founded in 1931 and was an important Afro-Brazilian organization. Similar to Afro-Cuban and Afro-Uruguayan organizations that operated in the same period, the Front struggled for the rights of Afro-Brazilians, who had in many instances lost out in the intense social competition wrought by the post-abolition immigration of millions of Europeans, Middle Easterners, and Japanese in the late 19th and early 20th century. The Front protested against racial discrimination by hotels, bars, clubs, and the police, and fought for the integration of Afro-Brazilians into Brazilian society and in legislative bodies, especially the National Congress.

The 1930s was a period of political polarization, with fascism and Communism at each end of the political spectrum, but nonetheless there were liberals in Brazil who opposed the Vargas regime. An example of a prominent liberal family was the Mesquita family, owners of the newspaper *O Estado de São Paulo* and representative of many in the São Paulo business establishment. Their newspaper was confiscated in 1940 by the Vargas regime and used to publish pro-government articles. In December 1945 it was returned to the Mesquita family.

The Vargas regime responded to the various oppositional forces it faced with a mixture of co-optation and repression. In 1933 it created the Special Delegation for Political and Social Security (DESPS, Delegacia Especial de Segurança Política e Social). It was a despotic regime, and the Chief of Police of the Federal District (then Rio de Janeiro) Filinto Müller was widely feared. It locked up and tortured thousands of political prisoners. While the regime built up the central state and extended its reach throughout the territory, its capacity was still quite limited. Repression, for example, was focused chiefly in the national capital and São Paulo. Brazil was still an agrarian society, and coercion was widely decentralized amongst landowners and subnational governments. The driver of the expansion of state power in this period was internal conflict rather than external warfare.

The New State, which took its name from the Portuguese authoritarian regime established in 1933, was the product of an auto-coup, or a coup by the president and his coterie against other centres of power within the state, on 10 November 1937. It lasted until 1945 and represents the most authoritarian phase of Vargas's first spell as president. After the auto-coup, the regime closed Congress, promulgated a new, authoritarian constitution, intensified censorship of the media, built up the armed forces, and stepped up repression, abolishing the Integralists, the Black Brazilian Front, and other oppositional organizations.

The double game and the Second World War

As the 1930s progressed, Brazil found itself caught between the opposing forces of fascism in Europe and Japan and the liberal democracies of Europe and the United States. The Vargas regime used ambiguity to try to get the best out of this situation. It signed a trade agreement with Nazi Germany which enabled it to trade coffee for industrial goods. It used this trade agreement to rearm and re-equip the armed forces. Many of the Vargas regime's top generals were sympathizers of Nazi Germany. At the same time

the Vargas regime maintained cordial relations with the
United States.

When the United States entered the Second World War on the
side of the Allies after Pearl Harbor on 7 December 1941, Brazil's
policy of ambiguity was no longer sustainable. Brazil broke
relations with the Axis powers in January 1942 and allowed the
United States to establish air bases in the north-east of the
country. The bases in Natal and Recife were crucial to the Allied
efforts to supply troops in North Africa. In the first part of 1942
German U-boats sank Brazilian merchant ships, causing the
deaths of hundreds of Brazilians. In August of 1942 Brazil
declared war on Germany and Italy.

Unlike other Latin American countries that stayed out of the
Second World War (Argentina, for example, only declared war on
the Axis powers in March 1945), Brazil sent troops to fight in the
conflict. The Brazilian Expeditionary Force (Força Expedicionária
Brasileira, or FEB) was a contingent of about 25,000 men sent to
Italy in 1944 to fight under the command of the US Fifth Army.
The FEB was an Army division that included infantry regiments
and artillery groups. It fought impressively in Tuscany and
Emilia-Romagna in 1944–5, at the Gothic Line, pushing the
Germans northwards. It captured more than 20,000 Axis troops
while losing almost 500 men with about 3,000 wounded.

The end of the war brought pressures for democratization in
Brazil. The FEB's role in the European theatre of the Second
World War was a reminder that the Allies had won in the name of
democracy and against the authoritarianism of the Axis powers.
Leading figures in the armed forces, which had grown in
autonomy and capacity during the war, decided to ease Vargas out
of the presidency. They allowed him to return to his ranch in Rio
Grande do Sul as a private citizen while the New State was
dismantled, replaced by a new democratic regime with a limited
franchise (illiterates, who were nearly half the adult population at

the time, could not vote) but one larger than that of the first republic of 1889–1930. General Eurico Gaspar Dutra, Vargas's Minister of War, ran for and won the presidency in 1945, serving as president from January 1946 to January 1951.

Vargas returns

Vargas, helped by his resourceful and perceptive daughter Alzira Vargas, who had stayed in the capital Rio de Janeiro, bided his time in Rio Grande do Sul and planned his return to power. Because his regime had institutionalized a new system of labour relations that recognized basic rights for workers, including the minimum wage, he was popular with the working class and trade unions. The consolidated labour laws, approved in 1943, were seen as an important achievement by many urban workers, although they were not consistently applied to rural workers. The franchise had also been expanded in the 1946 Constitution, giving many urban workers the vote for the first time.

Vargas had the benefit of two different party machines, the Social Democratic Party (PSD) that, despite its name, was a conservative party that appealed to landowners, industrialists, and the middle class and the Brazilian Labour Party (PTB), with its base of support in the trade unions. Running in a new guise as a developmentalist, Vargas won the presidential election of 1950 and returned to the presidency in 1951. It was during this period that the 'oil is ours' campaign, which had begun in the 1930s and was focused on retaining national control over oil reserves, gained an important victory. Petrobras, the national oil company, was created in 1953 with a monopoly on the production of oil and gas in the country. It is now one of the largest oil companies in the world, with considerable expertise in deep water drilling.

Other innovations that increased the state's role in the economy were taken during this second period of Getúlio Vargas in the presidency. The National Economic Development Bank, the

BNDE, was established in 1952. This bank was entrusted with the long-term financing of infrastructure and economic development projects across all sectors of the Brazilian economy. (In 1982 it became the BNDES, the National Economic and Social Development Bank.) Vargas used his presidency to praise and uplift Brazilian workers, employing a paternalistic ideology of 'workerism' that reinforced the president's image as the 'father of the poor'.

However, significant segments of Brazilian society were uncomfortable with the new incarnation of Vargas. Parts of the armed forces feared that the president's economic nationalism would put Brazil on a collision course with the United States (despite the fact that Vargas's foreign policy remained steadfastly pro-USA). Segments of the business community, especially those connected to the anti-Vargas Democratic National Union party (UDN), feared Vargas's pro-worker sentiments and the power of the trade unions. The journalist Carlos Lacerda, a member of the UDN, was a particularly fierce critic of Vargas.

On 5 August 1954, an attempt on the life of Carlos Lacerda in Rio de Janeiro led to the death of an air force major. The ensuing investigation uncovered links between the assassination attempt and Gregório Fortunato, President Vargas's personal bodyguard, and Benjamim Vargas, the president's brother. Amidst pressure for him to resign, Vargas committed suicide on 24 August, shooting himself through the heart in his bedroom in the presidential palace. A note said to have been written by Vargas and addressed to the Brazilian people was released to the press. It blamed the attacks on the president on international economic and financial 'forces' and 'interests' that did not want the Brazilian worker to be free or the country's people to be independent. Carlos Lacerda temporarily left Brazil amidst a wave of indignation at Vargas's death. Hundreds of thousands of people witnessed the funeral procession in Rio de Janeiro.

Fifty years in five

After an interregnum the presidency was won by Juscelino Kubitschek, a medical doctor from the state of Minas Gerais who had been a PSD mayor of Belo Horizonte, federal deputy for Minas Gerais, and governor of the same state. Kubitschek was able to navigate the political polarization of this period and finish his mandate, which lasted from January 1956 to January 1961. The era of President Kubitschek—or JK as he was known—is seen by many in Brazil as one of unique accomplishments. Kubitschek's optimistic slogan during his presidency was that Brazil would develop 'fifty years in five'.

The Kubitschek administration was able to realize some of the aspirations of the Vargas regime by continuing to industrialize the country. The growth of the automotive sector is an example of this. Some multinational automobile manufacturers such as Volkswagen and Mercedes Benz had already entered the domestic market in 1953. General Motors and Ford soon followed and in 1956 the National Association of Automotive Vehicle Manufacturers (Anfavea) was created. The region of Santo André, São Bernardo, and São Caetano near the city of São Paulo (known as ABC) became a centre for the manufacture of cars and trucks. The birth of the automotive sector in Brazil was an embodiment of the analysis of the UN Economic Commission for Latin America and the Caribbean (ECLAC), founded in 1948 and reflecting the idea of the Argentine economist Raúl Prebisch that development in Latin America could be achieved if imported manufactures were substituted by domestically produced items. This national developmentalist vision was supported by think tanks such as the Superior Institute for Brazilian Studies (Instituto Superior de Estudos Brasileiros, or ISEB) founded in 1955.

Several other developments added to the lustre of the Kubitschek period. In football, the Brazilian national team won the FIFA

World Cup for the first time in Sweden in 1958, with a 17-year-old Pelé scoring two goals in the final. Brazil had already made its reputation as a football powerhouse in the 1930s, but in 1950, when it hosted the tournament on home soil, it lost in the final to Uruguay in a defeat that was both unexpected and humiliating. The 1958 triumph, which Brazilians followed on the radio, went some way to ameliorating the mongrel dog complex. (Brazil's sporting reputation was further enhanced a year later when a 19-year-old from São Paulo, Maria Esther Bueno, won the women's singles title at Wimbledon on 4 July 1959.) Brazil went on to win the World Cup again in 1962 in Chile and in 1970 in Mexico, as well as in 1994 and 2002, consolidating its reputation not only as a country whose teams were successful, but as one that embodied a joyous and artistic approach to football, different from what was seen in Brazil as the relentlessly physical and mechanized European version of the game.

In music bossa nova, a fusion of American jazz and Brazilian samba, gained popularity. In 1958 the guitarist João Gilberto released the song 'Chega de Saudade' (Enough of Nostalgia) with music by Tom Jobim and lyrics by Vinicius de Moraes. The spare, understated style of bossa nova seduced many fans. Jobim and de Moraes went on to write 'Girl from Ipanema'. This song, which was performed by—amongst other artists—João Gilberto and his then-wife Astrud Gilberto, eventually became the best-known Brazilian song in the world. Bossa nova was played and imitated worldwide, attracting American musicians such as Stan Getz, Sarah Vaughan, Frank Sinatra, and Ella Fitzgerald.

Brazil also made its mark in this period in architecture and urban planning. President Kubitschek fulfilled an aspiration that had existed in Brazil at least since the founding of the republic and built a new capital, Brasília, in the interior of the country. The city was built in about three years by workers baptized *candangos* (a word of African origin meaning ordinary), many from the north-east of Brazil. It was inaugurated on 21 April 1960.

Located in the centre-west of the country, on the plateau of rolling hills called the *cerrado*, Brasília was designed by the urban planner Lúcio Costa in the shape of an aeroplane, with a central esplanade (the fuselage) crossed by two curved wings of housing and commercial establishments.

The period of the Kubitschek presidency was not without its difficulties. Kubitschek struggled to secure financing for his ambitious development goals and resorted to expanding the money supply, which fuelled inflation. JK only managed to temporarily paper over Cold War conflicts rather than overcome them. The benefits of growth were highly concentrated, and poverty and inequality were high, as the 1960 publication of the diary of a São Paulo favela dweller, Carolina Maria de Jesus, showed. Nevertheless, the JK years are remembered fondly by many Brazilians because they seem to represent a time when Brazil made its mark on the world stage. The industrial base was expanding and the population growing and concentrating in vibrant cities. In football, music, architecture, urban planning, and other fields of human endeavour Brazilians seemed to show that they could be different, self-confident, and creative.

Prelude to the coup

The 1960 presidential election was won by a mercurial politician called Jânio Quadros, who had been governor of São Paulo. The Quadros government struggled with one of the negative legacies of the JK years, high inflation, and also changed foreign policy in the direction of a more independent stance vis-à-vis the United States. The demonstration effect of the 1959 Cuban Revolution had a strong impact throughout Latin America. Cold War polarization intensified and Quadros's foreign policy, which included awarding Cuban revolutionary leader Che Guevara the National Order of the Southern Cross medal on 19 August 1961, caused discomfort in conservative business and military circles. When Quadros unexpectedly resigned on 25 August 1961, complaining about 'terrible forces' pressuring him in the presidency, parts of the armed forces rebelled against the idea that Vice-President João Goulart, a protégé of Getúlio Vargas, would assume the presidency. Goulart, who was in China at the time, witnessed from abroad a conflict between constitutionalist and rebel forces that was eventually settled by a compromise. In this deal, Brazil would change to a semi-presidential system, with a parliamentary-style cabinet, and Goulart would be allowed to assume the presidency.

This compromise did not endure. In a January 1963 plebiscite, Goulart won back full presidential powers. His presidency was marked by uncertainty and pressure from the United States and conservative forces inside the country. In a contentious move, Goulart applied the consolidated labour laws to rural workers and through his Minister of Labour Almino Afonso began to register rural trade unions. This ignited the opposition of landlords and Goulart's opponents, who feared that he would use the rural trade unions as vote banks for future election campaigns. Rebellions by enlisted men in the armed forces were not dealt with forcefully by the Goulart administration, invoking fears amongst the military high command. Many socially conservative forces including church and business leaders and middle-class representatives were concerned about a drift to the left by the Goulart government. On 19 March 1964 a March of the Family with God for Liberty took place in São Paulo, with tens of thousands of mostly middle-class people taking part. Twelve days later a military coup took place, with the support of the United States, and João Goulart fled to Uruguay, where he eventually died in exile.

The military coup of 1964 was a turning point in Brazil's political history. With the end of the presidency of João Goulart the Vargas era definitively came to an end. The conflicts that marked the era, between those who favoured and those who opposed a close relationship with the United States, and between those who favoured radical change, including redistribution to the poorest half of the population, and those who feared the instability this might generate, were resolved in favour of the pro-US and conservative forces.

Foundations of the modern state

The Vargas period was fundamental for modern Brazil because it laid the foundations for many of its institutions. The ideology of workerism was part of a labour system that involved the state, through the labour court system, mediating conflicts between employers and employees. During the Vargas era industrialization and urbanization accelerated, and a complex of state-owned firms such as the oil company Petrobras and the steel company CSN were created. The capacity of the central state was also enhanced through the development of a federal bureaucracy and the extension of state institutions throughout the national territory.

In the thirty-three and a half years between the 1930 revolution and the military coup of 1964, the idea of what Brazil was and could be also changed. New generations of politicians, writers, trade unionists, architects, artists, athletes, musicians, and journalists, amongst others, transformed what Brazilians and foreigners thought about Brazil. A new capital was built in the interior, and Brazil laid a claim to be an important modern country with a unique approach to life, the world, and resolution of the world's problems.

Chapter 4
Dictatorship and repression

Brazil experienced a twenty-one-year dictatorship from 1964 to 1985. Many countries in South America in the 1960s and 1970s experienced military rule, but the coup that created the Brazilian dictatorship in 1964 was particularly influential, spurring a cycle of other coups in the region, including in Argentina in 1966 and Chile and Uruguay in 1973. The subsequent regime in Brazil was also distinctive. This chapter will examine the authoritarian regime and its legacy in Brazil.

The coup was the result of tensions in the second republic of 1945–64. On one hand internationalists were on the side of the United States in the Cold War and the status quo domestically. This included most of the military high command, the leading business organizations, large landowners, most of the hierarchy of the Catholic Church, and the majority of the middle class. On the other hand many students, trade unionists, left party activists, and advocates of land reform wanted a more independent stance in the Cold War and redistribution and mobilization for change. Some on the left wanted Cuban-style Communism, while others preferred socialist or social democratic-inspired reforms.

On 31 March 1964, a military–civilian coalition initiated a self-proclaimed revolution that deposed the elected President

João Goulart (Figure 5). On 9 April the new government issued an 'institutional act' that overrode the 1946 constitution, purged the state apparatus (including the armed forces and Congress) of supporters of the prior government, organized investigations into alleged Communists and corrupt politicians, and laid the foundations for a dictatorship that was to become increasingly repressive. Through an indirect election in Congress, General Humberto Castelo Branco became president. Castelo Branco's initial aim might have been a relatively brief intervention to 'clean up' politics, eliminating alleged Communists and 'subversives', in order to hand power back to civilians in the presidential elections scheduled for 1965 (the first institutional act was due to expire on 31 January 1966, the scheduled end of Goulart's presidential term). However, he was outflanked by more hardline officers who were determined to keep the armed forces in control for a longer period of time.

5. A tank and soldiers being observed by onlookers in Rio de Janeiro during the military coup of 31 March 1964.

A variety of domestic and international factors came together to produce the coup. The main party on the right, the Democratic National Union or UDN, was losing voters in successive elections of the second republic, leading many of its politicians to call for military intervention. The coup was supported by the governors of São Paulo, Guanabara (as the state in which Rio de Janeiro is located was then called), and Minas Gerais, the three most important states in the country. Two of those governors were members of the UDN. Through the Superior War College, established in 1949 along the lines of the US Army War College, military officers gained an appreciation of the problems of the nation and a new confidence that they had the capacity to rule directly to try to address those problems. Goulart's permissive attitude towards revolts by enlisted men in the armed forces also gave the high command another, internal reason to oppose his presidency. And the Cold War context exacerbated the polarization within Brazil. The Cuban revolution had inspired the left and alarmed the right, and led the Brazilian military to strengthen its focus on enemies within rather than outside the national territory.

The role of the USA

President Lyndon Baines Johnson of the United States congratulated the new government on 2 April 1964, sending a telegram to the president of the lower house of Congress, the interim president of the country before Castelo Branco was sworn in. This recognition was quite early, leading to rumours of extensive US involvement in the preparation for the coup. Declassified documents show a clear US interest in deposing President João Goulart and support for the coup plotters. This interest began in the administration of Johnson's predecessor, President John F. Kennedy. The Kennedy administration was concerned about Goulart's tolerance of leftists in his cabinet and lukewarm support for the Alliance for Progress, the US programme for Latin America launched in 1961. Some Kennedy administration officials contemplated siding with the military in an attempted coup, but they feared the consequences of the military failing to do this successfully.

In 1962 President Kennedy sent Vernon Walters, a US Army officer who had worked with General Castelo Branco and the FEB in Italy during the Second World War and was fluent in Portuguese, to the US Embassy in Brazil to build better relations with the Brazilian armed forces. At the end of the year, in December 1962, President Kennedy sent his brother Robert Kennedy, then the US Attorney General, to meet with President Goulart in Brasília. From the Kennedy administration's point of view, the meeting did not go well. While Goulart tried to explain the delicacy of his political position, Robert Kennedy got the impression that he was trying to have his cake and eat it too, asking for US economic assistance but refusing to take US advice about the composition of his cabinet and the direction of his foreign policy.

US support for the coup included sending an aircraft carrier loaded with fuel and ammunition to Brazil in a manoeuvre dubbed Operation Brother Sam. Although the helping hand of Brother Sam was not actually needed, the implicit support might have galvanized the resolve of the coup plotters. US Ambassador Lincoln Gordon rationalized support for the military regime, claiming that the coup was constitutional because President Goulart had vacated his post. In fact Goulart had fled to Uruguay only when the scale of the military revolt became clear.

Conservative modernization

The military rulers cancelled the 1965 direct presidential election. They eventually promulgated a new constitution in 1967 with the consent of a controlled Congress. The 1967 constitution, revised substantially in 1969, concentrated powers in the hands of the executive and was even followed by the promulgation of secret institutional acts that had the force of law even though almost nobody knew what they were.

The military regime was a hybrid regime, in that it preserved more of the trappings of a democracy, including a functioning if restricted Congress and controlled two-party elections, than other similar regimes in the region. The regime excluded candidates it considered unreliable and changed electoral rules to suit its interests, but Congress operated throughout the dictatorship except for a few months in 1968–9 and two weeks in 1977. Furthermore, the regime's repression was relatively mild. The number of people who went into exile has been estimated at 10,000, and the total number of political prisoners at 25,000. Thousands of people were tortured, but a relatively small number of 434 killed and disappeared by the regime have been officially recognized by a truth commission that operated from 2012 to 2014. Although this is almost certainly an undercount, it is lower than the 20,000–30,000 and 5,000 people killed by the Argentine (1976–83) and Chilean (1973–90) authoritarian regimes, in estimates made by their respective truth commissions.

The Brazilian military regime was legalistic, using military courts to try suspects accused of violating the numerous and vague national security laws. These courts were integrated into the regular civilian system of justice and cases within them could be appealed to the civilian Supreme Court. Once registered in the system as defendants in military court cases, political prisoners were spared execution or disappearance, although they were still subject to torture. Acquittal rates were relatively high, and sentences averaged around four years. This was a very different approach to law from that of the Argentine junta of 1976–83, for example, which engaged in extra-legal disappearances on a large scale.

In the first four years, Brazil's authoritarian regime oversaw a process of conservative modernization of the economy. Foreign investment was welcomed and increased substantially. Multinational companies expanded their presence in the country. Inflation was subdued through a squeeze on wages. Trade unions were not abolished, but the leadership of the most combative unions was replaced by less recalcitrant leaders hand-picked by Ministry of Labour officials. Land redistribution was taken off the political agenda as the military regime tried to encourage the transformation of unproductive large estates into modern capitalist agribusinesses. Literacy programmes inspired by the ideas of the educator and philosopher Paulo Freire were closed down, while organizations advocating land reform such as the Peasant Leagues, prominent in the north-east, were abolished.

Nevertheless, in the cultural sphere, opposition to the military regime flourished. Demonstrations took place on the streets, including the famous March of the 100,000 on 26 June 1968 in Rio de Janeiro. Songs that were read as protests against the regime, such as Chico Buarque's 'Apesar de Você' (In Spite of You), released in 1970, were hugely popular. Theatrical groups such as the Arena Theatre Group staged plays with oppositional motifs and ideas. Journalists floated ideas contrary to those of leaders of the regime. Although in 1965 the regime banned all political parties and replaced them with the pro-regime National Renewal Alliance (ARENA) party and the officially permitted opposition, the Brazilian Democratic Movement (MDB) party, many informal political groups held meetings and discussed the political situation. Civilian politicians such as former President Kubitschek and former Guanabara governor Carlos Lacerda mobilized supporters.

Armed opposition to the regime emerged in 1966, when a bomb intended for then-minister of the army, General Artur da Costa e Silva, exploded in Guararapes Airport in Recife. The general was unharmed but two people were killed and fourteen wounded. Conflict between small groups of the armed left and the regime intensified. In September 1968 a federal deputy, Márcio Moreira Alves, angered the armed forces by suggesting that no one should attend the military parades on independence day (7 September) and that women should engage in a sexual boycott of military personnel (along the lines of the sex strike portrayed in *Lysistrata*, by the Greek playwright Aristophanes). When the regime tried to get Congress to strip Moreira Alves of his parliamentary immunity in order for him to be prosecuted, Congress resisted, and the regime closed down Congress in Institutional Act Number 5 (AI-5), promulgated on 13 December 1968.

AI-5 was a 'coup within the coup' which intensified the authoritarian characteristics of the regime and gave the executive extensive and unprecedented new powers. It gave the federal executive the power to intervene unilaterally in the state and municipal governments as well as to enforce preventive censorship of newspapers, television, films, music, and theatre. The act also eliminated habeas corpus in national security crimes, allowing the security forces to hold dissidents and suspected opponents indefinitely. The ten years during which AI-5 was in force was a decade in which Brazil was an outsider to the international human rights architecture then being constructed. Its regime was known abroad for its routinization of torture, its denial of political and civil rights, its limits on party competition, and its censorship and oppression of civil society.

Unlike other authoritarian regimes in South America, such as the Pinochet regime (1973–90) in Chile, the Brazilian military regime was not economically liberal. It was nationalist and developmentalist and promoted the expansion of state-owned firms. It used the power of the state to build up the country's communication, transportation, and energy infrastructure, laying telephone lines and building roads and dams. Under the auspices of the military regime the Rede Globo television network became the biggest in Brazil, with its influential news programmes and prime-time soap operas.

The high-water mark of economic development under the military regime was the period of the so-called 'miracle', the years 1969–73, when growth in GDP averaged 10 per cent per year. During these years opportunities for social mobility increased, although so did income inequality. For the rural poor opportunities for industrial employment offered the prospect of new lives in cities while for middle-class youth university places increased. Although President Emílio Garrastazu Médici (1969–74) was a dictator he was not unpopular, exploiting the victory of Brazil in the World Cup in Mexico City in 1970 and employing jingoistic language such as 'Brazil: Love it or Leave It' to celebrate the growth of a new 'Grand Brazil'.

The miracle did not last. The military regime was hit hard by the oil price rise of 1973–4 and sustained the economy for the rest of the 1970s by borrowing heavily in international markets. Like most of the rest of the region Brazil endured a recession in the early 1980s and subsequently experienced a 'lost decade', when the debt crisis exploded and per capita GDP stagnated.

Liberalization

The repression of the military regime reached its peak from 1969 to 1974, the so-called 'years of lead' (the same years as the miracle). Disappearances, executions, and torture took place amidst the clamp-down engendered by the passage of AI-5. A civil-military repressive apparatus, coordinated by the army, facilitated the search for and detention of suspected members of the armed opposition to the government. This was the period of the most daring actions by the armed left, such as when a group kidnapped the US Ambassador, Charles Burke Elbrick, in September 1969. Elbrick was let go in exchange for the release of fifteen political prisoners who were allowed to fly to Mexico.

In the early 1970s the Communist Party of Brazil, a Maoist offshoot of the Brazilian Communist Party, sent a group of armed militants to the Araguaia region of northern Brazil in what is now Tocantins state. Beginning in 1972 the army began to hunt this small band of about sixty guerrilla fighters with a force of 20,000 troops. By 1974 they had killed or captured almost the entire group. Today about fifty members of this group are considered disappeared. The defeat of the Communist Party of Brazil in Araguaia represented the end of the illusion on the left that the military regime could be defeated by the force of arms of an elite vanguard of young fighters. Henceforth groups on the left moved in the direction of organizing popular movements and were part of the redemocratization of the country in the second half of the 1970s and first half of the 1980s.

With the armed left defeated, the administration of President Ernesto Geisel, inaugurated in 1974, decided to embark on a policy of relaxation or liberalization. There were multiple reasons for this policy. Geisel was apparently concerned to rein in the security forces, who had acquired a great deal of autonomy and power in the repression of the armed left. The two-party system was also creating a situation in which each election was a referendum on the government, and the opposition MDB was gaining support in large cities such as São Paulo, Rio de Janeiro, and Belo Horizonte. During the course of the Geisel administration the president, aided by his chief of staff Golbery do Couto e Silva, engaged in a zigzag process of reforms that ended censorship, reached out to the moderate opposition, and eventually repealed AI-5. Geisel had to face down hardliners in some instances, such as when he fired the rebellious head of the army General Sílvio Frota in 1977.

Under Geisel's successor, President João Figueiredo, the Brazilian Congress in 1979 passed an amnesty law that freed most political prisoners, permitted the return of exiles, and extended a blanket pardon to any and all members of the state security forces that had engaged in torture, executions, and disappearances. This amnesty was a foundation of the conservative and gradual transition to democracy that took place in the 1980s. The regime also eliminated the controlled two-party system and allowed for multiple parties to be formed. In 1981 it survived a scandal when hardline members of the security forces accidentally exploded a bomb outside the Rio Centro shopping centre in Rio de Janeiro. The bomb was to have been placed in a concert hall and blamed on the left, thereby justifying the continuation of repression. In 1982 there were direct elections for governors in the states under the new multiparty electoral rules and opposition candidates won in several places.

In 1984 there were large marches and rallies demanding direct elections for president and an end to the authoritarian regime. Although the amendment in Congress to allow for direct elections failed, the protests showed the power of a newly aroused civil society and put pressure on the regime. In January 1985 in an indirect election in Congress Tancredo Neves, a long-serving politician, defeated the preferred candidate of the military regime, Paulo Maluf. Neves worked hard to reassure the military that there would be no prosecutions of military personnel for human rights abuses during the dictatorship. Neves fell ill on the eve of his inauguration and eventually died in April 1985. His vice-presidential running mate, José Sarney, a politician who had supported the military regime for most of his career, was sworn in as the first civilian president of Brazil since 1964 on 15 March 1985. Military rule was over.

In 1987 the Congress embarked on a process of devising a new constitution. The 'people's constitution' had an unprecedented amount of input from civil society, with many petitions delivered to Congress. In October of that year the constitution was ratified by Congress. It was an unusually long and detailed document, establishing many new rights, decentralizing the state to some extent, and seeking to avoid the abuses and distortions of the dictatorial period. Enforcement of many of the constitutional provisions proved to be difficult, and it was only slowly that much of the enabling legislation to make the constitution a living reality was passed.

In 1989 the first direct election for president took place since 1960. In the second round the contest was between Fernando Collor de Mello, the scion of a wealthy family from Alagoas in the north-east, and Lula, one of the founders of the Workers' Party (Partido dos Trabalhadores, PT) and a metalworker trade union leader from the industrial outskirts of São Paulo. In a close race Collor de Mello, supported by the Globo media conglomerate and most of the rest of the media, won and ushered in a new era in Brazil's politics.

Human rights

The repression of the military regime engendered domestic and transnational resistance. Exiles abroad alerted public opinion in Europe, the United States, and elsewhere about the routinization of torture. Non-governmental organizations such as Amnesty International and Human Rights Watch wrote reports on torture in Brazil; Amnesty's first was in 1972. Domestically, Peace and Justice Commissions were established under the auspices of the Catholic Church, and these followed various human rights cases and took part in the movement in favour of amnesty.

Several high-profile killings galvanized the human rights community. In 1973 a student at the University of São Paulo suspected of being a member of an armed left group, Alexandre Vannucchi Leme, was killed while in detention in São Paulo. The archbishop of São Paulo, Dom Paulo Evaristo Arns, held a mass for Alexandre at the cathedral in the Praça da Sé in the centre of the city, in defiance of the authorities. In 1975 a journalist, Vladmir Herzog, was called into a detention centre to be interrogated and was found hanged in his cell, supposedly as a result of his committing suicide. Few people believed the official account of his death, and again Dom Paulo Arns held a mass for another prominent victim of the regime's repression. In 1976 a metalworker, Manoel Fiel Filho, was killed in circumstances similar to those of Vannucchi Leme and Herzog. This case led to President Geisel firing the commander of the Second Army in São Paulo, General Ednardo D'Ávila Mello. These emblematic cases, part of a larger pattern of state violence directed at students, journalists, and workers, generated mobilization, criticism, and resistance, and sometimes this resistance led to changes at the level of the regime.

In the early 1980s some former political prisoners began to direct their attention to the prison conditions of ordinary criminals and the inquisitorial, unequal, and at times brutal treatment of suspects in the Brazilian criminal justice system. In the ensuing decades a strong network of human rights organizations was built up. Brazil ratified all the major human rights treaties once it had restored its democracy and every democratic administration in the period 1989–2016 made some improvement in the state's human rights institutions.

The new unionism and new social movements

Civil society mobilization was an important factor in the evolution of the regime's policy of liberalization into one of democratization. A significant part of this mobilization was carried out by the trade unions. A new trade union movement, one critical of the populist and elite-controlled unionism of the second republic (1945–64), emerged at the end of the 1970s. The metalworkers' union in the ABC region of greater São Paulo, led by Lula, went on strike in 1978 because it was revealed that the government's estimate of inflation, which was used to regulate pay increases in the labour courts, significantly understated the real rate of inflation.

The 1970s and 1980s saw the emergence of other new social movements. Feminist movements questioning gender inequality, Afro-Brazilian movements criticizing prejudice and demanding racial equality, neighbourhood associations in poor urban communities, indigenous movements fighting for cultural survival and rights to ancestral land, proto-LGBTQ+ movements affirming the right to different sexual orientations, and movements of rural workers and the rural poor seeking opportunities to cultivate the land and become small farmers, all of these and more emerged from the process of liberalization and democratization of the authoritarian regime.

Authoritarian legacies

Comparing the New State of 1937–45 with the dictatorship of 1964–85 gives an insight into the way the state had developed over the three decades that separated the two regimes. The dictatorship of the 1960s and 1970s was bureaucratic and national in a way that the New State was not. Its repression was coordinated and sophisticated. It promoted the integration of the national territory in ways that would have been unthinkable to rulers in the 1930s.

The legacy of the Brazilian dictatorship seems to be very different from the legacies left by similar regimes in the region such as those in Argentina (1966–73 and 1976–83), Chile (1973–90), and Uruguay (1973–85). In the latter countries there was a gradual movement to repudiate the dictatorship. Extensive transitional justice uncovered and in many cases punished those responsible for human rights abuses. Politicians embraced a post-authoritarian view of the need for a combination of liberal guarantees of minority rights and democratic commitment to majoritarian decision-making. And the commanders of the armed forces issued apologies for the role of the armed forces in the repression.

In Brazil, in contrast, a significant part of the population regarded the dictatorship as having been both economically successful and politically legitimate. The hybrid nature of the regime, the fact that it kept Congress open for most of the time and had elections (albeit indirect ones for the presidency and governorships) and a functioning judiciary meant that the Brazilian dictatorship was accepted by many as not only consonant with Brazilian political traditions, but as a necessary force to prevent the ascension of a Communist government in the country. The industrialization that had taken place under military rule and the fact that Brazil became a top ten economy during this period were also used by supporters of the regime to praise authoritarian rule. This helps to explain how a candidate who openly expressed admiration for the dictatorship, Jair Bolsonaro, won the presidency in 2018. No similar candidate has won the presidency in Argentina, Chile, or Uruguay since the end of authoritarian rule.

On 31 March 2019, on the fifty-fifth anniversary of the coup, a video was released by the presidential palace. The video included a presenter who spoke the following lines: 'The Army saved us. The Army saved us. This is undeniable. And all of this happened on a common day like today, the 31st of March. You cannot change history.' The video was also disseminated by one of the sons of the president, federal deputy Eduardo Bolsonaro, with this commentary: 'On a day such as this one Brazil was liberated. Thank you armed forces of 64! Ask your parents or grandparents who lived in that period how it was!' Two and a half months later, the then-minister general Carlos Alberto dos Santos Cruz said in the Senate that the video was released due to a mistake made by a palace functionary who received the video on WhatsApp and thought it had something to do with pension reform.

Despite the explanation, the fact that the video had been circulated by the president's staff gave the impression that the government endorsed this view of the coup. For a democratically elected government, this was paradoxical. It suggests the enduring appeal in Brazil of an authoritarian approach to government, a repressive orientation that violates human rights but 'gets things done'. Such an approach is complemented and supported by elements of a hierarchical and unequal society in which violence is an intrinsic part of the maintenance of order. This is problematic for the strengthening of democracy. Before analysing the progress and challenges of democracy in Brazil, we will look at the economic trajectory of the country.

Chapter 5
Rich country, poor people: economic challenges

In 1988 members of the rural trade union in Itambé, near the border with Paraíba in the north-eastern Brazilian state of Pernambuco, lived hard lives. They cut sugar cane during the harvest, from September to February, but were often unemployed during the fallow season in between. So the trade union offered them a special service. It provided them with coffins, built by hand in a workshop alongside the union offices. Many of these coffins were for babies and small children, reflecting the high infant mortality rate in the area.

In those days sugar was the mainstay of Pernambuco's economy. The state did not have a broad economic base. But today, about half an hour by car from Itambé, there is a Fiat-Chrysler factory that makes the Jeep Renegade and employs 9,000 people. In Cabo, south of the state capital Recife, the Brazilian company Gerdau has a steel plant. In Jaboatão, just next to Cabo, the steel company Arcelor Mittal, whose CEO is the Indian businessman Lakshmi Mittal, has a distribution centre. Pernambuco also has a textile sector and petrochemical plants in the port of Suape. In Recife the Porto Digital, a digital hub, produces computer software. The economic base of the state has been industrialized and digitalized. There is still poverty, but the rural workers' union in Itambé probably does not need to offer children's coffins to its members any more.

This anecdote reflects the fact that Brazil is one of the most successful examples of 20th-century industrialization in the world. In one brief part of that century, from 1965 to 1980, its industrial output quadrupled, while Japan's tripled during the same years. It is now an upper middle-income country that is part of the BRICS association of five major emerging economies (Brazil, Russia, India, China, and South Africa). In the 1990s and 2000s, Brazil also made impressive strides reducing infant mortality and poverty, increasing life expectancy, achieving universal primary school enrolment, increasing access to higher education and technical training, and building an extensive social safety net that includes a public health system and a conditional cash transfer programme called Family Allowance. Brazilians now have more access to food, education, health care, and full-time, formal sector jobs than they did in the 1980s.

Brazil could eventually become a high-income country. However, there is a problem. As Matthew Taylor argues, Brazil is now caught in a low-growth trap. Brazilian per capita GDP growth was 1.2 per cent per year between 1985 and 2017. The average for upper middle-income countries during the same period was 5.6 per cent, while the global average was 1.9 per cent. From 1985 to 2017 upper middle-income countries' share of Brazilian per capita GDP rose from 37 per cent to 76 per cent, showing that Brazil has been losing ground economically to competitors. Brazil is also one of the ten most unequal countries in the world. Income inequality dropped by about 12.5 per cent from the period 1985–9 to the years 2010–16, but in the same era it dropped by about 15 per cent in Chile and 20 per cent in Peru. Productivity in manufacturing and services is low, as are savings and public investment in infrastructure. Industry has shrunk as a proportion of the total economy and the country has become more reliant on commodity exports.

The Brazilian economy reflects a paradox. While the well-being of most people in the country has improved over the last three decades, the productive base that sustained that improvement is under threat. This chapter will examine the achievements and challenges of the economy from several angles.

A mid-20th-century industrializer

The Great Depression plunged Latin America, Brazil included, into a crisis in which earnings from exports plummeted, foreign exchange was scarce, and previously imported products began to be produced domestically. In 1931 the federal government created the National Coffee Council to maintain the price of Brazil's chief export at that time, mainly by buying and burning part of the harvests. In 1933 the government established the Sugar and Alcohol Institute to regulate the production of sugar and alcohol (ethanol) derived from sugar throughout the country. These institutions are examples of the intertwining of the state and private sector in Brazil.

As time went on the emergency measures taken in the 1930s crystallized into a set of ideas, known as developmentalism, that justified Brazil's stance towards the world economy. Developmentalists argue that the opportunities facing late developers are different from those that faced early developers and that this justifies deviation from liberal orthodoxy in economic policy in areas such as capital mobility, trade, investment, and the provision of credit. They also assert that many currently rich countries did not adhere to liberal orthodoxy in the early stages of their industrialization. For developmentalists, the state should not passively adhere to liberal or 'free market' prescriptions, but instead actively provide protections, subsidies, and other incentives to steer firms in directions that they might otherwise avoid. In this way development policy can reallocate capital, shift the composition of investment, adapt new technologies and management practices, and increase comparative advantage in strategic industries.

The major institutions of Brazil's developmental state were built during and after the Second World War. These include the national development bank, the BNDE, now the BNDES, in 1952, to provide credit to companies and help build infrastructure, the establishment of the state oil company, Petrobras (Figure 6), in 1953, with a monopoly on oil production, and the National Steel Company (CSN), created in 1941 (and privatized in 1993). Others include the national mining company CVRD established in 1942 (privatized in 1997), the CNPq, the National Council for the Development of Science and Technology, created in 1951 and part of the Ministry of Science and Technology, CAPES, part of the Ministry of Education and established to finance the further education and training of university personnel, established in 1951, and FINEP, a state bank to finance science, technology, and innovation, established in 1967.

A complement to the institutions above is the 'S' system, a set of nine federal institutions financed by private sector companies to train workers in various sectors of the economy. SENAI was formed in 1942 and trains workers in industry; SENAC provides training for workers in retail and services; SENAR, created in 1991, provides professional education for rural workers; SENAT, created in 1993, provides professional education for transport workers; while SEBRAE provides support to small and medium-sized firms. The state companies mentioned above and the 'S' system form a panoply of state institutions that established deep roots in the private sector in Brazil, establishing a variety of capitalism quite different from that found in the Anglo-American world.

An agricultural and mining heavyweight

Brazil began its colonial existence as a plantation economy and those origins still influence its development. Land in Brazil has traditionally been not merely a factor of production but a reward for service and proximity to power, as well as a foundation for the

6. The headquarters of the Petrobras oil company, a major part of the Brazilian economy, in Rio de Janeiro.

accumulation and maintenance of more power and privilege. This power includes the ability of large landowners to direct the legal and coercive apparatus of the state in their region. It also entails landlord control over and obligations to dependants among the rural poor. In colonial and imperial Brazil land was almost unlimited. What really mattered for production was control over labour. From the perspective of landlords, workers always posed the threat of desertion, moving to the hinterlands to try to farm on their own, so labour controls were often highly coercive, even with workers who were not slaves but merely tenants or sharecroppers.

The original division of the colonial land grants or *capitanias* among a handful of friends of the king reflects this reality. The captains or rulers of these large land grants had near absolute powers in their territory, including the right to inflict capital punishment on subjects. The result was a highly concentrated system of landholding. In Brazil, unlike for example the United States, the state's exclusionary tendencies were not mitigated in later stages of development by frontier policies that granted land to the landless. Whereas the Homestead Act of 1862 granted frontier land to anyone willing to settle in the USA, Brazil's 1850 Land Law prohibited the acquisition of public land by any means other than purchase, thus putting an end to previous rights to gain land through occupancy.

Brazilian policies in agriculture promoted conservative modernization. Unlike Latin American countries such as Mexico and Bolivia, Brazil never had a political rupture that weakened the landed oligarchy and allowed large-scale redistribution of land to those who cultivate it. The brief period of mobilization around land and labour issues in the late 1950s and early 1960s which saw the emergence of rural trade unions was ended forcefully by the military coup in 1964. The military regime of 1964–85 subsequently imposed policies that essentially took land redistribution in already settled areas off the political agenda. Government policies of subsidized credit (mainly for large producers), tax breaks, price supports, and other incentives promoted the development of large, highly capitalized, mechanized farms and ranches, many of them producing for export. This conservative modernization created an exodus from the countryside, as sharecroppers, tenants, and small farmers lost access to land, and rural workers lost jobs.

At the same time that land concentration was taking place, new, previously unused lands were passing into private hands. In the 1970s alone private landowners acquired, by purchase and government grants, some 31.8 million hectares of previously public land. This happened especially in the west and north of the country. To minimize potential social unrest in the face of these policies, the military regime initiated programmes of rural social assistance (pensions and health) as well as colonization (mostly in the Amazon region).

On one level government policy in agriculture was successful. Brazilian agriculture is one of the most dynamic and productive sectors in the world. It has benefited from scientific research that has helped to adapt crops and cultivation techniques to the soils and climatic conditions prevalent in the country. Much of this research has been carried out by Embrapa, Brazil's agricultural research agency located in the Ministry of Agriculture.

Brazil is a top producer of coffee, soybeans, sugar, tobacco, fruit and vegetable juices, cotton, beef, chicken, pork, and ethanol produced from sugar. Agriculture is highly globalized, accounting for almost half of Brazil's exports, and the agricultural sector is sometimes called the 'green anchor' of the economy. This strong performance has been achieved with far fewer subsidies than those that prevail in the United States, the European Union, and Japan. Brazil still has a land frontier and has potential for further expansion of its agricultural production. The agribusiness sector also has a major impact on Brazilian foreign policy and was a factor in the negotiations between the European Union and Mercosur (a trade bloc integrating the economies of the region) that led to the signing of an important trade agreement, after twenty years of talks, between the two blocs in 2019. To go into effect the deal must be ratified by the blocs' member states, and Austria, Ireland, and France have voiced objections to it.

Agriculture's growth and development stands in contrast to the shrinking of the manufacturing sector in recent decades. In 1980 manufacturing was about a third of GDP, whereas in 2019 it was only 16 per cent. During the same period manufactured goods as a share of exports fell from 59 per cent to 40 per cent. Much of this deindustrialization has to do with the rise of China and other low-cost Asian manufacturers. These exporters have established inroads in supply chains involving Brazilian industry and have also eaten away at Brazil's market share of industrial goods exported to southern South America, the region in which Brazilian manufactured goods are most competitive. Brazil's loss of competitiveness in industry has been attributed to many factors, including relatively high labour costs, poor infrastructure, a lack of skills in the workforce, a cumbersome system of taxation that is onerous and difficult to comply with, and an oligopolistic structure in many sectors that does not stimulate improvements in management and production techniques.

The mining sector has been important in Brazil since the 18th century. Brazil is the second largest producer of iron ore in the world, but also produces minerals that are important to metalwork, steelmaking, and the production of fertilizers and petrochemical products. It produces, for example, manganese and niobium, important alloys of steel in products such as gas pipelines. Recent mining disasters have brought attention to the sector. In 2017 the Samarco dam in Minas Gerais, owned by Vale and BHP Billiton, burst, allowing contaminated water to surge along the Rio Doce (Sweet River), killing nineteen people and leaving a path of devastation in its wake. In 2019 a similar disaster at Vale's Brumadinho dam was worse than the Samarco tragedy in terms of lives lost, with over 200 dead and eleven disappeared.

Growth with social inclusion

In 1994 the Real Plan stabilized the Brazilian economy and brought to an end years of chronic inflation. Annual price increases dropped to a low single figure and Fernando Henrique Cardoso, who had been the Finance Minister when the Plan was carried out, won the presidency. In his two terms in office from 1995 to 2002 Cardoso maintained price stability and also increased social spending, beginning a process that gradually began to reduce poverty. This safety net was expanded in the 2000s under the presidency of Cardoso's successor, Lula (2003–10).

Perhaps no programme epitomizes the Lula administration's commitment to social inclusion as much as the Family Allowance (Programa Bolsa Família or PBF), one of the largest conditional cash transfer programmes in the world. The result of a fusion and expansion of existing programmes and begun in 2003 in the first year of Lula's presidency, the Family Allowance now includes roughly 14 million families comprising 49.6 million people, or 26 per cent of Brazil's population. The programme reaches beneficiaries in 99.7 per cent of the 5,570 counties (*municípios*) of Brazil. Like other conditional cash transfer programmes (CCTs), the Family Allowance involves a cash transfer, a targeting mechanism, and conditionality. Payments are made on the basis of a vast database called the Cadastro Único para Programas Sociais (CadÚnico) or the single registry for social programmes. CadÚnico contains data on 23 million low-income families.

Families are eligible for the PBF if their income falls below a certain threshold. Payments vary depending on family profiles. Average payments are modest and despite the vast scale of the programme, it costs only about 0.5 per cent of GDP. This amounts to less than 3 per cent of total social spending in Brazil or one-tenth of the money spent every year servicing the government's debt.

The conditionality of the Family Allowance concerns schooling and health. Beneficiary families must keep their children aged 6 to 15 in school for 85 per cent of the annual school days (this drops to 75 per cent for those aged 16–17). They must also get their children younger than 7 the inoculations required by the national immunization schedule and allow the growth and development of their children to be monitored by professionals in the national health service. Pregnant women and nursing mothers aged 14 to 44 who are beneficiaries of the Family Allowance also have to agree to periodic monitoring by a health care professional.

The creation of the Family Allowance programme was part of an extraordinary period of growth with inclusion in Brazil. From 2003 to 2011, Brazilian per capita income increased 40 per cent while income inequality fell by almost 10 per cent. The incomes of the bottom decile rose much faster than the incomes of the top decile. The poverty rate fell from 37.13 per cent in 2003 to 21.42 per cent in 2009. In absolute terms, from 2001 to 2007, the population living in extreme poverty (with monthly per capita income below R$70, or roughly US$16) fell by 11 million people, while the number of people living in poverty (with monthly per capita income below R$150, or about $34) declined by 13 million. From 2003 to 2015, the number of people in the so-called 'class C'—a marketing category consisting of those with a monthly family income between R$1,000 ($228) and R$4,000 ($910)—rose from 66 million or 38 per cent of the population to 120 million or 60 per cent of the population, becoming a majority. Commentators began to analyse the emergence of Brazil's 'new middle class'. Some hailed the new middle class as the harbinger of a major transformation in Brazil, while others argued that it was actually a new working class.

The Family Allowance was not the principal cause of these economic changes. The drop in income inequality in Brazil in this period was caused by a variety of factors. According to one study, about half of the change was caused by increases in non-labour income, including transfers such as the Family Allowance. The other half came from social and economic changes such as increases in access to education and the expansion of the formal sector labour market. The steady increase in the minimum wage was also significant.

Unfortunately the severe recession of 2015 and 2016 reversed the positive inroads Brazil had been making in poverty and income inequality reduction. According to the World Bank, the number of Brazilians living below the poverty line rose from 17.9 per cent in 2014 to 21 per cent in 2017.

Although the progress made in the 2000s was considerable, it does seem to have been contingent on favourable circumstances, including high commodity prices. At the end of 2016 the Brazilian Congress passed a constitutional amendment (number 95) freezing the federal budget in real terms. While this amendment does not in and of itself solve the problem of gradually increasing federal spending—other reforms are necessary for that—it is a reminder of how limited the federal government's ability to affect poverty levels is. The coronavirus pandemic and consequent drop in economic activity in 2020 also hit the economy hard. In the second quarter of 2020, the unemployment rate was around 12 per cent, while the economy was projected to shrink by 7.7 per cent during the year.

Mercosul and the BRICS

In 1991 Brazil signed the Treaty of Asunción with its neighbours Argentina, Paraguay, and Uruguay. This marked a major change in Brazil's orientation to its region and marked the beginnings of Mercosur (in Spanish; Mercosul in Portuguese). The most important relationship for Brazil within Mercosur is with Argentina. Trade between Argentina and Brazil increased during the 1990s and many firms began to produce in both markets. Despite tensions between the two countries caused by volatility, for example when the Brazilian currency—the 'real'—lost value at the beginning of 1999 and when Argentina defaulted on its sovereign debt in 2001, this trade relationship remains important to both countries.

In 2001 a report by economists at Goldman Sachs identified Brazil, Russia, India, and China as the biggest and most important emerging markets in the developing world. The BRIC acronym, initially just an investment category for clients of an investment bank, became a concept that seemed to capture the increasing multipolarity of the global order. In 2009 Russia organized the first BRIC Summit and in 2011, at the request of China, South

Africa was included in the annual summits, which became BRICS summits that year.

While Brazil's growth rate does not match those of China and India, and China is clearly the dominant economy and state in the group (with an economy more than five times as big as Brazil's, and per capita GDP over 90 per cent of Brazil's), being part of the BRICS is important to the managers of the Brazilian state. In 2015 the BRICS created the New Development Bank to fund infrastructure in the developing world, and this bank (through the BNDES, which is a partner) has lent to some projects in Brazil. While the BRICS group does not seem to want a radical reform of the global economic system, Brazil's membership of it allows it to nurture a strong trade relationship with China and balance its dependence on trade with the European Union and the United States.

The fiscal crisis of the state

Brazil has a structural problem when it comes to state spending. Over 90 per cent of the federal budget in 2019 was obligatory spending, expenditure that was constitutionally mandated, including transfers to state and local authorities. The pension system for state employees, including judges and former legislators, accounted for 44 per cent of the federal budget that year. Pensions at the top end of the civil service are extremely generous. Public pensions, welfare payments, and other transfers amount to 23 per cent of GDP. A series of reforms are needed to reduce the fiscal deficit.

The tax system is cumbersome to comply with and complicated. Some analysts argue that the country has no room for more taxation, as tax revenue is about a third of GDP, well above the Latin American average of 23 per cent. But the tax system is regressive. Roughly half the tax revenue collected in Brazil is levied on consumption in value added taxes. Tax as a percentage of income tends to be higher amongst the poor than the rich in Brazil. The poor can end up paying as much as half their income in tax. Income tax, meanwhile, is capped at 27.5 per cent in Brazil (compared to 45 per cent in the UK and 37 per cent in the USA), while many independent professionals pay only 15 per cent.

Taxation on wealth is also low. For example, Brazil's federal government limits the tax rate on inheritance to 8 per cent (compared to 40 per cent in the UK above a £325,000 threshold and above $11.2 million in the USA). Taxes on land and property are also relatively low. Furthermore, as various anti-corruption investigations have revealed, tax evasion by the wealthy, who have access to sophisticated financial instruments and offshore accounts, is a serious problem.

Liberal and developmentalist prescriptions

Brazil's idiosyncratic model of capitalism suffers from various disabilities. Savings between 1985 and 2017 averaged 17.6 per cent of GDP against a peer group average of 29.8 per cent. Productivity in manufacturing and services has been stagnant (although it rose in agriculture). The quality of basic education is low and skilled labour in many sectors is in short supply. The Brazilian economy has grown mainly by doing more of the same rather than innovating. Brazilian firms have a comparative advantage in sectors that are commodity-producing, labour rather than skills intensive, and of a fairly low level of complexity. Brazil is still important industrially, producing cars, airplanes, pharmaceuticals, chemicals, and other goods, but much of this is assembly, with research and development done elsewhere. But it seems to be unlike more disciplined developmental states, such as those in East Asia (e.g. Japan, South Korea, and Taiwan), in which the state is often able to impose conditions on industries that benefit from state support. Brazil, where state guidance is weaker, does not seem to be moving up the value-added ladder by producing more high-technology goods.

The liberal recipe for Brazil is to plunge the country into a 'competitiveness shock' by simplifying and reducing the tax burden, lowering tariffs and exposing the domestic economy to international competition, privatizing state-owned enterprises, abolishing the national development bank (BNDES), flexibilizing the labour market to allow for easier hiring and firing, and 'capitalizing', essentially privatizing, the pension system. For liberals the great improvement in the Brazilian economy was the Real Plan, begun in 1994, because it initiated a period of fiscal responsibility on the part of the state. In their view, rigorous exposure to the harsh winds of market competition and a downsizing of the state will dynamize the economy and produce a higher rate of growth, more rapid job creation, and innovation on the part of entrepreneurs.

While the idea that suppliers in perfectly competitive markets have incentives to produce goods and services efficiently at low prices makes logical sense, it is unclear that a competitiveness shock would induce a positive response from Brazilian businesses. Many businesses operate in oligopolistic sectors—areas of the economy dominated by a few large firms that are able to determine prices—in which incentives to improve have been scarce. A rapid and unilateral opening up of the economy could lead to foreign exporters capturing domestic market share, leading to further deindustrialization of the Brazilian economy. And the liberal idea that the national development bank 'crowds out' domestic lenders makes sense when the economy is at near full employment, but is not applicable when there is slack capacity and high unemployment, as there was in 2020.

The liberal 'competitiveness shock' advocated by some is popular in public discourse. But it is unclear how many people in Brazil, aside from US-trained economists in some universities, really want thoroughgoing reform in this direction, as was carried out, for example, in Chile after 1973 or in Mexico after 1982. Business groups, especially industry, do not seem keen to throw off the shackles of state tax breaks, subsidized credit, tariff barriers, and other forms of protection that allow them to profit without heavy foreign competition in a large domestic economy. Even if orthodox liberal prescriptions could dynamize and improve the Brazilian economy—and there is considerable doubt about whether they would—public support for such reforms is weak. It is also unclear whether a competitiveness shock sufficiently brutal to have a deep economic impact could be undertaken under democratic conditions. The Chilean and Mexican reforms mentioned above took place under authoritarian and semi-authoritarian conditions respectively.

Public opinion polls in Brazil show widespread support for state guidance of the economy. A 2007 poll, for example, showed that a majority of Brazilians thought privatizations had been on the whole negative (62 per cent agreed, 25 per cent did not). Fewer than three out of ten Brazilians surveyed in 2018 agreed that the partially state-owned oil company Petrobras should be fully privatized. A Datafolha survey conducted in 2017 revealed that 76 per cent of those interviewed believed that the responsibility for generating prosperity lies with the government.

The developmentalist perspective differs from the liberal one. The problem from this point of view is that the developmental state is not robust enough to fend off capture by private sector groups. What developmentalists want is a coordinated set of public policies and public spending to lead private sector investment into strategic sectors, areas of the economy in which Brazil can begin to move up the value-added chain into high technology and state-of-the art manufacturing and service provision.

If a turn in the direction of full-blown liberal 'shock therapy' is unlikely in Brazil, so is a refinement of the tools of the developmental state in order to produce a more disciplined and strategic version of state-guided capitalism. That is because the political model for a more high-powered developmental state seems to be lacking. A strong executive able to delegate to a capable bureaucracy exists, but there is insufficient political insulation from the private sector. The state can discipline labour, but it cannot discipline capital. Instead, it is permeable and porous, liable to capture by private firms with promiscuous and at times illicit relationships with state managers, in a way that makes subordinating economic activity to a long-term strategic framework impossible. Furthermore, the Brazilian state is dependent on foreign investors to make up the gap between the savings rate and the capital needed for investment. State managers are reluctant to steer too far away from liberal orthodoxy for fear of scaring off these foreign investors. It is therefore likely that Brazil will continue with a hybrid set of economic policies, a mixture of liberalism and developmentalism, one that fully pleases neither liberals nor developmentalists.

On the other hand the Brazilian economy possesses some advantages that bode well for its future. It still has a large frontier of arable land and could increase its agricultural production without destroying the environment. It is a water superpower, with abundant supplies of both 'green' water (rain absorbed by plants) and 'blue' water (rivers, lakes, and groundwater). Brazil has the largest proven reserves of oil in South America outside Venezuela, and it has accumulated about $350 billion in foreign reserves, making it less vulnerable to global economic volatility than in the past. And if the tendency towards 'deglobalization' continues—a trend away from the integration of national economies due to declining levels of foreign investment and trade, which some analysts argue began after the financial crisis of 2008–9 and which has been exacerbated by the coronavirus pandemic in 2020—Brazil should be more insulated than many other national economies due to its size.

Economic challenges

While Brazil's developmentalism as practised by governments during the second republic (1945–64) and military regime

(1964–85) achieved relatively high levels of growth, the more recent developmentalism of the democratic era has not. Furthermore, its version of developmentalism lacks genuine strategic guidance by the state. It is instead marked by state 'followership' or capture of parts of the state by large private sector firms, as revealed by the Carwash corruption scandal.

Although there is strong dissatisfaction in Brazil with its idiosyncratic model of statist development, including complaints about the high and complicated tax burden, the low quality of public goods, the prevalence of corruption, and the lack of responsiveness of the political system, it is not easy to see how change will occur. The state is capable of transformation: the 1994 Real Plan and the 2003 implementation of the conditional cash transfer programme Bolsa Família are evidence of that. However, to adjust the development trajectory requires a strong and stable political coalition that is united on macroeconomic policy. Such a consensus is absent. Instead, political polarization has widened in recent years.

Brazil faces another dilemma. For over a century Brazilians expected their country's population to keep getting bigger, and it did. It grew steadily from about 17 million in 1900 to the present population of about 210 million. But Brazil's birth rate is 1.77 trending towards 1.70, which is below the replacement rate and below the world average of 2.5. Projections suggest that Brazil's population could peak at 233 million in the middle of the 21st century and then (in the absence of large-scale immigration) start to decline. Furthermore, the 'demographic dividend'—a situation in which the number of people of productive working age is increasing faster than the increase in the number of dependants (children and old people)—will end quite soon. In fact, the IBGE, the Brazilian Institute of Geography and Statistics, claims that it ended in 2018.

Brazil could be heading towards a disappointing future in which the end of the demographic dividend, an economy incapable of generating high growth, and the uncertainties and costs of climate change produce a generation with a much lower standard of living than that of its predecessor. It would be better if Brazil's development aspirations could be realized and the country could continue to improve economically while reducing inequality and poverty. But if not, Brazil could remain a rich country with many poor people. A lot will depend on whether the political system can adapt in order to meet the demands of the citizenry, a topic to which we now turn.

Chapter 6
Democratic development or decay?

On 27 October 2002, after running unsuccessfully in 1989, 1994, and 1998, Lula won the second round of the presidential election with 61 per cent of the eligible vote. The result demonstrated the resilience of Brazilian democracy by showing that, seventeen years after the end of the dictatorship, a candidate of a centre-left coalition could compete for and win the presidency. Lula's personal history was unlike that of any previous Brazilian president. Born to an impoverished family in the interior of Pernambuco in the north-east, Lula migrated to greater São Paulo, where he became a metalworker and later a trade union leader and founder of the Workers' Party.

Lula's election in 2002 began a thirteen-and-a-half-year period in which politicians from the Workers' Party controlled the presidency. The contested history of these years helps to explain much of the current polarization in Brazilian politics between a new ideological right and the left. This chapter begins with a basic description of the political system and then examines the accomplishments and failures of the Workers' Party in power, paying attention both to the reduction of poverty and to the opportunities for reform that were missed, as well as the revelations of corruption that occurred. It then moves on to the political crisis that began in 2013 and contributed to the election of Jair Bolsonaro in 2018.

The system

Brazil has a presidential and federal political system with a
directly elected president who serves a four-year term with the
possibility of one consecutive re-election. The lower house of
Congress represents the people on the basis of population, with a
minimum of 8 and a maximum of 70 seats per state, for a total
of 513 seats. The Senate allots 3 seats to each of the 26 states
and the Federal District of Brasília for a total of 81 seats. There is
separation of powers between the Congress, executive branch,
and the judiciary. The judiciary is represented at its apex by eleven
Supreme Court justices who are appointed by the president and
approved by the Senate and serve until they turn 75. State
governments are run by directly elected governors and state
legislatures and municipalities are run by directly elected mayors
and municipal councils. Brazil's constitution is lengthy, with nine
major sections and 250 highly detailed articles. Amending the
constitution requires two votes of three-fifths of both houses of
Congress. As of early 2020 the constitution had been amended
105 times in thirty-two years, for an average of more than three
amendments per year.

The party system is complicated. There are thirty parties in
Congress. Despite the fact that voter identification with parties is
very weak, aside from those who identify with the Workers' Party,
and politicians switch parties frequently, using them as convenient
vehicles for their campaigns, candidates must have a party
affiliation to run in an election. This eliminates the possibility of
independent candidates and puts the leaders of political parties
in the national Congress firmly in control of the rules of the
electoral game.

In 2015 the Supreme Court ruled that businesses were no longer
allowed to donate to election campaigns. In response Congress
expanded the electoral fund of public money allocated to parties

for their campaigns. Parties have to obtain a minimum of 1.5 per cent of the national vote (or elect lower house deputies from nine different states) to qualify for access to the electoral fund and free television and radio time during the campaign. This threshold is scheduled to rise to 3 per cent by 2030 and, starting in 2020, parties will no longer be able to form alliances with other parties with whom they do not share a platform. The growth of Brazil's political parties may have peaked, but it has peaked at a level that still makes Brazil an extreme case of multipartyism, with the most fragmented party system of any major democracy in the world.

Brazil has a gender quota in its elections, like many other countries. Political parties are required to make sure that at each election, 30 per cent of their candidates for office are women. Passed in 2000 and later revised, the law has not had the impact on representation that some reformers had hoped for. After the 2018 elections, women held 15 per cent of the seats in both the Senate and the lower house. This compares unfavourably to countries in which more than 40 per cent of the seats in the national legislature were held by women in 2019; these include Bolivia, Costa Rica, Sweden, Mexico, South Africa, Rwanda, Finland, and Norway. The impact of the electoral gender quota has been limited for several reasons, including the tendency of male party leaders to place women in races they are unlikely to win and to siphon off their finance for other campaigns.

Candidates for the lower house of the national Congress, as well as state deputies, win elections on the basis of open-list proportional representation with states as districts. This means that voters across the entire state choose from the same list of candidates. Candidates in the same party effectively run against each other. The average state electorate is 5 million people, so the distance between voters and their Congressional representatives is large. Senators are elected using a simple majority system. Brazilian political campaigns are expensive. In the 2018 election, candidates spent more than R$2 billion (about US$455 million) on radio, television, and print advertising.

Representation in the lower house of Congress is not reapportioned on the basis of the census every ten years and is highly unequal. While the most populous state, São Paulo, has one lower house deputy for every 664,000 citizens, Roraima, the smallest state, has one for every 64,000 people. As in Australia and some other democracies, voting is mandatory in Brazil. Unlike many other democracies, rates of voting are roughly equal across the different levels of income in the population and across the regions of the country.

Since 1994 presidential, gubernatorial, and legislative elections at the state and federal level have concurred, strengthening the alignment between national and subnational election outcomes. Because the winner of the presidential election has to win 50 per cent or more of the vote in either the first round or a second-round run-off, presidents often make an effort to build broad nationwide coalitions that enable them to start their terms with popular majorities and a mandate that gives them leverage over Congress. But because of party fragmentation, the president's party has never had a majority of the seats since 1990. Hence presidents try to manoeuvre within a system that has been described as coalitional presidentialism. They build coalitions of disparate parties in Congress in order to pass their legislative agenda. Presidents tend to placate the members of their coalitions by awarding them ministerial positions (sometimes with the right to appoint large numbers of people at lower levels of the ministry) and budget amendments that send federal resources to their home states.

The Lula years

The period 1995–2010 was remarkable for its relative stability and social inclusion. It was in this period, and especially during Lula's two terms 2003–10, that observers began to praise the vibrancy, innovation, and expansion of citizenship rights within Brazilian democracy. The main axis of Brazilian politics ran between the centre-right PSDB (Brazilian Social Democracy Party) and the centre-left PT (Workers' Party). The two parties agreed on many things, including the need for macroeconomic stability and social inclusion. Both ruled through pragmatic alliances with conservative political parties and politicians, making coalitional presidentialism work in their favour.

Economic stability and fiscal responsibility constituted the foundation of this achievement. Stability was based on a tripod of three key economic policies: a floating and primarily market-driven exchange rate, a primary fiscal surplus (a surplus before the payment of interest on debt), and the control of inflation within a band of 2.5 to 6.5 per cent per year. The success in maintaining these policies and the durability of the Real Plan are reflected in the fact that although there were thirteen finance ministers between 1985 and the end of 1994, there were only three between 1995 and 2010.

Brazil's institutions of accountability and transparency were also strengthened from 1995 to 2010. The Public Ministry, a prosecutorial service charged with protecting the public interest and forming a virtual fourth branch of government, gained new powers in the 1988 constitution. The federal controller general (CGU), a key rule-maker and supervisor of the bureaucracy, was created in 2001 and the TCU, the federal Audit Court, was strengthened in the 2000s. The Supreme Court acquired greater autonomy from the executive and legislative branches. The Federal Police gained resources, staff, autonomy, and prestige as well.

Brazilian democracy experimented with innovations in participation and social policy. Participatory budgeting, initiated by a Workers' Party municipal government in Porto Alegre, Rio

Grande do Sul in 1989, spread to many other cities within and outside Brazil. The idea of participatory budgeting was to submit parts of the municipal budget to deliberation by members of communities. Residents could meet, for example, and decide how their share of the municipal budget could be spent in their neighbourhood. The idea generated some controversy because it overlapped with the traditional mechanism of representation on the city council, but it was integrated with the latter in that the city council still had overall control of the municipal budget.

Participatory budgeting was accompanied by other innovations in participation. Health and education councils were created at the local level to allow democratic input into the management of these key public services. At the federal level under Workers' Party administrations, national councils were set up to channel input from a variety of civil society organizations. Connections between social movements, NGOs, and the state were strengthened in a variety of ways, from environmental and indigenous policy to women's rights and racial equality. Innovations in social policy included the Family Allowance conditional cash transfer programme.

The Lula government of 2003–10 achieved many successes. The economy grew at an average of 4 per cent per year while poverty fell. The number of formal sector jobs expanded. The Lula government invested heavily in universities and technical education, increasing the number of students in both areas. For students from low-income families, programmes such as Pro-Uni financed the cost of their education in private universities. Affirmative action for Afro-Brazilians and the indigenous, as well as students from state high schools, was introduced at many universities in the 2000s (and became mandatory for federal universities in 2012). In the 2006 election the base of support for the Workers' Party changed, reflecting the impact of these policies. The party lost much of the middle class but gained many new poor voters.

Lula was re-elected in 2006 despite a corruption scandal, the *mensalão* or big monthly payment, in which members of the government were accused of paying members of allied parties to vote for their bills in Congress. Lula's political capital was probably at its peak in his second term; he was popular and commanded a national party with considerable administrative capacity. But he also had to deal with a fragmented and conservative Congress. The debate about what the Lula administration could or should have done is contentious. However, criticisms include a relative neglect of basic education (relative to higher education); insufficient attention to the quality of other public goods such as transportation and health; a lack of reform of the tax system, particularly its complexity and regressive nature; and ineffective promotion of science, technology, and industry. Serious political reform was also avoided, as were attempts to address the structural causes of economic inequality and the economy's lack of dynamism.

Dilma Rousseff

At the end of his second term Lula hand-picked his successor, a technocrat called Dilma Rousseff who had been his minister of mines and energy and then chief of staff. Dilma had no experience of running for elected office and Lula's success in getting the Workers' Party to ratify her nomination demonstrated his high degree of personal control of the party. Dilma lacked Lula's ability to communicate with the public and build political coalitions. Nonetheless, Lula was able to transfer his popularity to her, and she was elected Brazil's first woman president in 2010.

In its first two years, the Rousseff administration was fairly popular. The economy was still growing. However, the growth model inherited from the Lula administration proved unsustainable. The expansion of low-productivity service sectors reduced competitiveness and the rising minimum wage increased public spending because pensions were linked to the minimum wage. The government's efforts to increase the purchasing power of poor households were not accompanied by a corresponding investment in public goods such as education, health, and transportation. In the absence of deeper structural reforms and in a context of declining commodity prices, Rousseff presided over a widening public sector deficit and eventually a full-blown recession in 2015–16, when the economy shrank by almost 7 per cent.

In June–July 2013 a series of protests rocked the country and set off a political crisis from which the Dilma Rousseff administration never fully recovered. The demonstrations began in São Paulo over a 7 per cent rise in the metro and bus fares, but morphed into a more general national protest coinciding with the start of the Confederations Cup, the warm-up to the FIFA World Cup scheduled to take place in Brazil the following year. While the protests were diffuse, a common complaint amongst the largely young and relatively well-educated protesters was that while the government was building 'FIFA-standard' football stadia, it was not investing in schools, hospitals, public transport, and public security systems of an equally high standard.

The June–July 2013 protests were the largest in a generation. At their peak on 20 June they involved an estimated 2 million people in over 400 cities. They signalled the existence of a wide gap in trust between Brazilian citizens and their elected representatives. The protests were a surprise to many and a signal that all was not well with Brazilian democracy.

Inside the carwash

Legislative changes were an important prelude to the uncovering of the biggest corruption scandal in Brazil's history. A popular signature-gathering movement succeeded in pressuring Congress into passing an anti-vote-buying law in 1999. In 2010 Congress responded to another popular campaign by passing a clean file (*Ficha Limpa*) law, prohibiting candidates who have been convicted on appeal to the justice system from running for office. New money laundering, anti-racketeering, and plea-bargaining laws were also passed by Congress. Brazil also joined the OECD Anti-Bribery Convention in 2000 and Congress passed the Clean Companies Act in 2013, imposing higher penalties on people in companies convicted of engaging in bribery, contract rigging, clandestine campaign finance, and other illicit acts.

Assisted by some of this new legislation, investigators uncovered an enormous kickback scheme in Petrobras, the state-controlled oil company, in March 2014. In the Petrolão, as it was dubbed by the press, large construction firms colluded in their bids for contracts with the company, systematically overcharged for the work obtained through the contracts, and funnelled the extra money back to Petrobras executives as well as politicians and political parties. The heart of the Carwash investigation, as it has been called, was a task force in Curitiba headed by then federal judge Sérgio Moro. Task forces were also established in Brasília, São Paulo, and Rio.

The Carwash investigation involved a careful division of labour between the federal judiciary, prosecutors in the Public Ministry, the Federal Police, and the tax authorities. It is one of the largest anti-corruption probes in the world, involving hundreds of searches and arrests, almost 200 requests for international cooperation, multiple charges being brought against hundreds of defendants, and in some cases the recovery of stolen assets. High-profile targets of the investigation include former presidents Lula and Michel Temer, former Rio governor Sérgio Cabral, former president of the lower house Eduardo Cunha, and the former CEO of the Odebrecht construction company Marcelo Odebrecht.

Carwash became popular with many in Brazil because it appealed to the principle of equality before the law and the idea that powerful politicians and corporate executives should receive the same treatment for wrongdoing as ordinary citizens. Whereas in the past, Federal Police investigations involving a politician were usually sent by judges to the Supreme Court, where they were effectively archived, in the wake of the new anti-corruption laws, politicians became real targets of investigations. Amongst jurists, however, Carwash is controversial because some see it as inquisitorial, giving federal judges too much power to indefinitely detain suspects and compel witnesses to testify in return for reduced sentences.

When he was a federal judge, Sérgio Moro had both a judicial and a political strategy. Judicially, he was known for fast work and tough sentencing, as well as the creative interpretation of statute. Politically, he stimulated the support of social movements and politicians on social media and carefully courted the press, providing journalists with bite-sized summaries of his judgments and a ready supply of opinions.

Carwash reflects the fact that as tolerance of corruption has declined and accountability institutions have been strengthened in Brazil, the state has split, and gone to war with itself. The institutions entrusted with investigating corruption have removed members of the executive and legislative branches, as well as executives in major companies, in a slow but deliberate manner. What this means for the governability of the country and the legitimacy of its political institutions is uncertain. Carwash is part of a judicial system that gives wide-ranging and sometimes arbitrary power to individual judges, including Supreme Court judges, and which is sometimes lacking in consistency and predictability. Carwash could come to be seen as a major change in Brazilian history, a process that moved the country towards a new equilibrium in which impunity for corruption is no longer the norm. But it could also be seen, like the Clean Hands investigation in Italy in the 1990s, as a temporary aberration that changed little in the long term.

Impeachment

While Dilma Rousseff survived the June–July 2013 protests and won re-election in 2014, her second term was overshadowed from the start by attempts to undermine her authority. In February 2015 she lost control of the lower house of Congress when a political adversary became president of that body, and by December of 2015 the same lower house president had initiated a charge of impeachment against Rousseff.

The impeachment took nine months. The charge made against Rousseff was that she had authorized delays in payments to state banks in order to make the fiscal deficit look smaller than it actually was. This charge was technical and similar manoeuvres had been used by other elected officials, although perhaps not on the same scale. No charges of personal corruption were made against the president. On 17–18 April 2016, the lower house of Congress voted on whether to refer the case to the Senate; 367 deputies voted in favour, with only 172 against. The then deputy Jair Bolsonaro dedicated his vote in favour of impeachment to Carlos Alberto Brilhante Ustra, an army intelligence officer and notorious torturer of political prisoners during the dictatorship. After the lower house vote President Rousseff stepped aside, provisionally replaced by her Vice-President Michel Temer. On 31 August, after several days of deliberation, the Senate voted 61 to 20 to remove the president from office. In an unexpected twist, the Senate brokered a deal in which Dilma Rousseff would not lose her political rights for eight years as required by the constitution. The Temer administration was born amidst acrimony and mutual recriminations, with a formal mandate until the end of 2018. President Temer had very low approval ratings and his government's main legislative actions were to flexibilize some of the labour laws and remove the requirement of 30 per cent Petrobras participation in all offshore oil drilling. After being accused of corruption in May 2017, Temer's focus narrowed to self-preservation. He clung to office and reached the end of his mandate facing multiple charges of bribe taking and money laundering.

Impeachment is always a political act, and this one was supported by wide swathes of the population, but its legitimacy was debatable. It weakened the presidency, involved a highly selective invocation of the rule of law, and did not address the problem of systematic corruption amongst the major parties and in Congress. Testimony leaked from the Carwash anti-corruption investigation suggested that many politicians in Congress were involved in the Petrobras kickback scheme, and their desire to impeach the president was linked to their attempts to shield themselves from investigation and prosecution.

Public insecurity

One of the potential benefits of democracy is a reduction in violence. Unfortunately Brazilian democracy has not enjoyed this benefit. While the Truth Commission created by the Rousseff administration identified 434 deaths and disappearances under military rule in its 2014 report, that was a small fraction of the annual homicides in the country during that decade. Police violence was part of that picture—almost 11 per cent of the killings in 2018, for example, were perpetrated by the police. The homicide rate almost tripled between 1980 and 2018, from 11.7 per 100,000 in 1980 to 27.5 in 2018. In 2017, 17 of the 50 most violent cities in the world were in Brazil.

Brazil's steep social inequalities and high rate of violence, including police violence, result in a democracy in which the effective exercise of rights by many poor citizens is limited (see Figure 7). Marginalized populations face frequent violence from organized criminal groups, as well as the police, who often obtain impunity when they kill in the line of duty, especially in favelas or in remote rural areas. In the greater metropolitan region of Rio de Janeiro alone, an estimated 2 million people live in communities dominated by *milícias*, groups of former and current police personnel who use their power to extort money from residents, while others live under the control of drug traffickers. Violence in these areas is not necessarily a product of a lack of state capacity, but of political arrangements that leave these areas

7. **The BOPE (special operations police unit) of the state military police training in the metro in Rio in preparation for the Olympic Games of 2016.**

vulnerable to coercion. Coercion by different organized criminal factions also exists within prisons, not only to impose order internally but to conduct business outside the prison walls. Brazil's more than 700,000 prisoners constitute the third largest prison population in the world after those of the United States and China. An estimated 40 per cent of these prisoners are awaiting trial.

The inequalities of the criminal justice system, in which the wealthy hire expensive lawyers who can make numerous appeals and keep their clients from definitive judgment, while the poor go to overcrowded and dangerous prisons, is a reflection of the larger social inequalities in which the system is embedded. Furthermore, journalists, human rights activists, social movement leaders involved in land disputes, and other critics of the status quo can be subject to retaliatory killings, as the 2018 assassination of Marielle Franco, a city councillor and critic of the *milícias* and the police in Rio, shows.

The 2018 election

In January 2018, a federal court in Porto Alegre upheld Judge Moro's conviction of former President Lula for taking a bribe and money laundering, and increased the sentence from 9 years and 6 months to 12 years. Lula began serving his sentence in Curitiba on 7 April 2018. Lula's lawyers later appealed to the Supreme Court, arguing that Lula should be released so that he could run for the presidency. Polls showed Lula to be the leading candidate, with support of about 30 per cent of the electorate. When the Supreme Court ruled against Lula in September 2018, the Workers' Party made Fernando Haddad, a former Minister of Education and mayor of São Paulo, its candidate on the last day that it was allowed to do so, 10 September 2018.

Another development also changed the presidential race. Candidate Jair Bolsonaro was stabbed at a campaign rally in Juiz de Fora, Minas Gerais on 6 September. Bolsonaro was rushed to São Paulo for emergency surgery. Although he had taken part in debates on 9 and 17 August, he did not participate in all subsequent and proposed debates. Instead he continued his campaign on his own terms, giving television interviews and posting content on Facebook, Twitter, and WhatsApp.

Bolsonaro, a former army captain who had been a deputy in the national Congress for twenty-seven years, and represented the small Social Liberal Party (PSL), ripped up the rule book for a presidential campaign. He had very little free television and radio time and raised a relatively small amount of money. The demonstration effect of Donald J. Trump winning the presidency of the United States in 2016 helped him. In Fernando Haddad of the Workers' Party he had the opponent that he most wanted. In the first round on 7 October 2018 Bolsonaro got 46 per cent of the vote to Haddad's 29 per cent, almost winning the election outright (eleven other candidates split the rest of the votes). And on 28

October 2018 he won the second-round run-off by 55 per cent to Haddad's 45 per cent of the valid votes.

Bolsonaro claimed to be a critic not just of the thirteen and a half years of rule by presidents from the Workers' Party from 2003 to 2016 but of the entire gamut of democratic governments since 1985. These supposedly 'centre-left' governments had engaged in the politics of horse-trading and log-rolling characteristic of coalitional presidentialism. Associating this form of politics with the corruption uncovered by various investigations, Bolsonaro praised the military dictatorship, called the Workers' Party and the left 'Communist', and in a series of comments criticized the environmental movement, human rights campaigners, the LGBTQ+ community, Afro-Brazilian activists, and feminists. The latter were accused of promoting a nefarious 'gender ideology' that supposedly undermined traditional gender roles. Despite the fact that many found his language offensive, Bolsonaro's narrative wove together anti-establishment and anti-PT sentiments in a way that resonated with many in the electorate.

Bolsonaro's slogan 'Brazil above everything, and God above everyone' combined nationalism and popular religiosity with a populism that divided the country between a pure people and a corrupt, irreligious, self-serving, and 'Communist' elite. The idea that many of the nation's ills such as endemic corruption, high rates of crime and violence, underperforming schools, a stagnant economy, high unemployment, and poor public services could be blamed on the Workers' Party seemed to appeal to at least some of Bolsonaro's voters. Indignation about corruption, fear of rising crime and violence, and evangelical Christianity were also part of the newly resurgent ideological right that helped to elect Bolsonaro. The ideas of the Brazilian Olavo de Carvalho, an astrologer and self-styled philosopher who lives in Richmond, Virginia in the United States, were also influential on the Bolsonaro campaign and subsequent government.

After Bolsonaro's election, Judge Sérgio Moro accepted the president-in-waiting's invitation to be the next minister of justice. This raised doubts as to the impartiality of Judge Moro in the case against Lula. The doubts were amplified in June 2019 when *The Intercept*, an online publication founded by the journalist Glenn Greenwald, published hacked or leaked messages on a private communication system between Sérgio Moro, when he was a federal judge, and Deltan Dallagnol, a prosecutor in the Federal Public Ministry. Although the publication of these messages was criticized and their interpretation contested, they suggested that Moro colluded with the prosecutor against Lula and in other ways stacked the deck against defendants in his court. On the 24 April 2020, Moro resigned as Minister of Justice when he clashed with President Bolsonaro over the replacement of the Director General of the Federal Police. Moro, a symbol of the fight against corruption for many, remains a potent political force, and a potential rival of President Bolsonaro.

A new kind of government

There are different centres of power within the Bolsonaro administration. These include the inner circle of the president's family, including his three sons Congressman Eduardo Bolsonaro, Senator Flávio Bolsonaro, and Rio City Council member Carlos Bolsonaro; neoliberal reformers at the Economics Ministry; the team focused on corruption and organized crime at the Justice Ministry; and the armed forces, led by Vice-President Hamilton Mourão and the head of Institutional Security General Augusto Heleno. The latter group is a formidable presence; nine of twenty-two ministers come from the military, more than in any government during the dictatorship, and there are hundreds of members of the armed forces in lower-level political appointments in the executive branch.

Whether the Bolsonaro administration poses a threat to democracy is debated in Brazil. One set of arguments centres around the role of the military. Some argue that military members of the cabinet and administration have generally been responsible and respectful of civilian and popular supremacy over democratic institutions. Others feel that the strong military presence in the cabinet is dangerous in a country that had a military regime as recently as the 1980s. They fear that the military participants in the administration could be dragged into political conflicts, especially when President Bolsonaro tries to mobilize his base against the Congress and judiciary, and that this could threaten both civilian control over and the impartiality of the armed forces. Others argue that the military has used its position within the cabinet and upper echelons of the administration to defend its corporate privileges, as when it secured a special deal on pension reform and maintained a relatively generous defence budget.

There are different concerns about whether the president's populism, which is intolerant of pluralism and impatient with liberal institutions, is a threat to democracy. When the president's son Eduardo said in an interview on 31 October 2019 that if there were widespread protests in Brazil the government might have to enact a new Fifth Institutional Act, he was condemned by other political actors, including the lower house president Rodrigo Maia. However, the comment was consistent with the paranoid tendency amongst some supporters of the Bolsonaro administration. Other observers worry less about the Bolsonaro family and more about the effect of Bolsonarismo on society. In particular they point to pro-Bolsonaro militants who use offensive language in aggressive attacks on independent journalists, artists, activists, and critics of the Bolsonaro administration on social media platforms.

The debate about democracy also focuses on a group of highly ideological ministers, some admirers of Olavo de Carvalho, who control policy in key areas. These ministers are sometimes accused of being against the rights won by different segments of the Brazilian population since the return to democracy in the 1980s.

For example, Damares Alves, the minister of women, the family and human rights and an evangelical pastor, attacked gender equality as an ideology that stimulates domestic violence in March 2019. Alves has also said that her personal preference is that abortion should be illegal under all circumstances (abortion is legal in Brazil only to save a woman's life, in cases of rape, or when the foetus has anencephaly, a fatal absence of a major portion of the brain, skull, and scalp).

Concerns about the impact of the Bolsonaro government on democracy include the government's commitment to anti-corruption investigations and possible links between the president's family and *milícias* in Rio de Janeiro. To give one example in which these concerns were raised, on 19 December 2019 prosecutors in Rio de Janeiro revealed that the president's son Flávio Bolsonaro had deposited R$1.6 million in a bank account linked to a chocolate shop that he owns in Rio between 2015 and 2018. The prosecutors believe that this was money laundered after it was kicked back from his employees' salaries when Flávio was a state legislator in Rio (a practice known as *rachadinha*, to share something by breaking it into portions). This investigation dents the anti-corruption credentials of President Bolsonaro and enhances the perception that the Carwash anti-corruption investigation is not a priority of his government. It also could unearth evidence of ties between the president's family and *milícias* in Rio, because two of the people employed by Flávio were the wife and mother of Adriano da Nóbrega, an ex-captain of the BOPE (Special Operations Battalion) of the Rio de Janeiro military police who was thought to have commanded a death squad in Rio and who was killed by police in Bahia on 9 February 2020.

The administration has emphasized religious social conservatism, violent policing, anti-environmentalism, economic liberalism, and a pro-Trump foreign policy. Consistent with its commitment to neoliberal reform, it abolished the Ministry of Labour, moving its functions to various other ministries. The environment minister set about immobilizing the federal government's forest protection infrastructure and announced that he intended to reduce the size of and allow economic development projects in indigenous reserves. He replaced the staff of the Chico Mendes Institute of Biodiversity Conservation (ICMBio) and clipped the wings of IBAMA, the forest protection agency, limiting its ability to levy fines for illegal deforestation. Money collected for the latter plummeted.

The administration's biggest legislative success of its first year was passing pension reform at the end of October 2019, a change projected to curb the growth of the public debt, which hovered around 79 per cent of GDP at that time. The government's response to violence and crime has been to pass legislation at the end of 2019 that widens the scope under which legitimate self-defence can be invoked by police who kill in the line of duty. The president in office showed himself to be relatively uninterested in coalition-building in Congress, which he delegated to the lower house president Rodrigo Maia. Instead he remained in campaign mode by engaging in culture wars, whipping up outrage against supposed threats to family values and national order. In November of 2019 he announced that he was leaving the PSL and creating a new party, the Alliance for Brazil.

On 30 April 2019 the then minister of education Abraham Weintraub announced a 30 per cent cut in the non-salary component for federal universities. This came after he threatened to cut the budget of three federal universities for promoting *balbúrdia* (disorder). On 15 May 2019 there were major protests in Brazilian cities against the budget cuts and in defence of public higher education (see Figure 8). Counter-demonstrations in defence of the government and its proposed reforms, on a significant but somewhat smaller scale, took place on 27 May. The battle lines over higher education were drawn, with the government alleging that there was an ideological bias in the universities and its critics

8. **Protests against the government's cuts to the budgets of federal universities and to research scholarships, Paulista Avenue in São Paulo, 15 May 2019.**

seeing the government as reflexively against education and research.

In 2019 an international conflict broke out over fires in the Brazilian Amazon and evidence that rates of deforestation had increased significantly from the year before. President Bolsonaro threw petrol on the flames of the controversy by disputing the accuracy of the data produced by his government's Space Institute (INPE) on 19 July 2019 and firing the head of INPE Ricardo Galvão, a physicist with a Ph.D. from MIT, on 2 August, after he defended the quality of the data. This firing was criticized by the Brazilian Association of Science and the Brazilian Society for the Progress of Science. On 27 August President Bolsonaro refused an offer from the G7 countries of $22 million to fight the fires. A survey released by IBOPE in mid-August found that 96 per cent of those interviewed agreed that President Bolsonaro and the federal government should do more to prevent illegal deforestation in the Amazon.

On 8 November 2019 Lula left prison in Curitiba after a Supreme Court ruling that defendants cannot be imprisoned until all of their appeals have been exhausted. In his speech to supporters after his release, Lula lamented Brazil's economic and social conditions, and said that he planned to tour the country and oppose the Bolsonaro government. Electoral challenges to the Bolsonaro government are likely to centre around the economy, as in the case of the Workers' Party, or in terms of the perceived need to restore civility to public discourse. They may also focus on the consequences of President Bolsonaro's contrarian handling of the coronavirus pandemic, when he minimized the threat of the virus and criticized the quarantines imposed by many governors and mayors and supported by Health Minister Luiz Henrique Mandetta, whom Bolsonaro fired on 16 April 2020.

Democracy in the balance?

The transition of the 1980s produced the longest period of democracy in Brazil's history, and political institutions are functioning. The period of stability and consensus of 1995–2010 produced steady improvements in the quality of democracy, and Lula's election in 2002 inaugurated a period of growth with inclusion. But the health of democracy has been increasingly questioned in recent years. Since June–July 2013 words such as crisis, impasse, and stagnation have been used to describe the political system. With the passage of time the period of stability and consensus has been forgotten, and the achievements of the Lula administration (2003–10) in reducing poverty have been overshadowed by criticisms of its corruption and lack of more thoroughgoing reform. The corruption was not new or exclusive to the PT, but it took place under a party that once prided itself on an ethical approach to politics. Survey evidence suggests that satisfaction with democracy in Brazil is low. In 2018 only 9 per cent of Brazilians surveyed said that they were satisfied with the performance of democracy, a drop of 40 percentage points from 2010 and the lowest rate of satisfaction in Latin America. Even the judiciary, an important actor in politics, is viewed with scepticism by many Brazilians.

Coalitional presidentialism is still the only game in town for Brazil's president and members of Congress, given the reality of party fragmentation. The Bolsonaro administration's attempts to play by different rules did not succeed, and it reverted to the old pattern of negotiation and deal-making to get its desired legislation passed. Brazil awaits reforms that can bring the system of political representation more closely into alignment with the rest of society, bridging the gap in legitimacy and trust that currently exists between elected officials and citizens.

The majority of Brazilian voters opted for change in 2018. But it is unclear what sort of change the election represents. The Workers' Party is still a strong electoral force, especially in the north-east. The year 2018 could be a single deviant election or it could create a new, long-term cleavage in the electorate between the new ideological right and the left, in the same way that the PSDB–PT cleavage divided the electorate in the 1995–2010 period, albeit within a much narrower ideological range than the one that exists today. Alternatively, a centre–right coalition could emerge to contest these two opposing forces. It is also not clear to what extent Bolsonarismo will remain a personalistic movement or instead become an institutionalized force channelled by the Alliance for Brazil or some other political party. What is likely is that polarization and questions about its health will continue to mark Brazil's democracy in the years to come. If it is any consolation, that is the condition of many other democracies around the world.

Chapter 7
Brazil and the multipolar world

On 2 January 2019, Ambassador Ernesto Araújo gave his inaugural address as Brazil's minister of foreign relations in Brasília. During his speech of a little more than half an hour, the bespectacled and bearded diplomat said, 'For a long time Brazil said what it thought it must say. It was a country that spoke to please the administrators of the global order. We wanted to be a good student in the school of globalism, and that was all . . . But Brazil has once again begun to say what it feels and feel what it is.'

In his speech, Araújo mentioned individuals and countries he looks up to. The individuals included President Bolsonaro, inaugurated the day before, and Olavo de Carvalho. With regard to countries, Araújo said, 'we admire the USA, those who raise their flag and revere their heroes . . .We admire those who struggle against tyranny in Venezuela and other places. For this reason we admire the new Italy, for this reason we admire Hungary and Poland, we admire those who affirm and not those who deny. The world's problem is not xenophobia but oikophobia—from oikos, oikía, the home. Oikophobia is the hatred of one's own home, one's own people, one's own past.'

Standing at a podium in front of a multi-coloured tapestry by the artist and landscape architect Roberto Burle Marx, the new foreign minister continued his speech. 'There is a horrendous, shocking theophobia in our culture. Not only in Brazil, but in the whole world. A hatred of God, and we know where it comes from, it is channelled by the codes of thought and non-thought that make up the global agenda. To destroy humanity it is necessary to finish with nations and separate man from God, it is this which they are attempting, and it is against this that we are rebelling.'

Araújo's speech bewildered many diplomats in the Brazilian Foreign Ministry and was analysed and debated by journalists in newspapers published the following day. It went against many long-standing conventions of Brazil's Foreign Ministry, often called Itamaraty after the palace in Rio de Janeiro that used to be its headquarters. Rather than recognize the global order as something that Brazil helped to construct, and that it wants to work well, the speech assumed that there is a conflict between Brazil's national interests and those of 'globalism' or the 'global agenda'. Its praise for other countries was limited almost exclusively to those that in January 2019 had governments led by illiberal national-populist leaders and parties. And in mentioning not only nationalism but God, the speech defied Brazil's tradition of the separation of church and state, which began with the first republic in 1889.

This chapter puts the speech into context by examining Brazil's foreign policy tradition. It looks at some of the main ideas in that tradition and then describes Brazilian contributions to global politics in areas such as international development, the environment, security, and global health. It then focuses on the rupture promoted by the Bolsonaro administration in 2019.

Brazil's foreign policy tradition

Brazil has a strong diplomatic tradition that emphasizes moderation, the peaceful resolution of conflicts, and Brazil's ability to seek consensus by maintaining dialogue with almost all other states. Brazil's key characteristics are its isolation from the centres of global power and its condition as a developing country. In consonance with these conditions, the thread of continuity in Brazilian foreign policy is the concern for autonomy in order to pursue national economic development. Brazil usually positions itself in favour of moderate reform of the institutions of global governance and as a gentle critic of the inequalities and injustices of the international system.

Like its former colonizer Portugal, Brazil is a country with relatively weak armed forces that must rely more on guile than strength. This involves a search for alliances and reliance on information, well-prepared briefs for negotiators that include persuasive arguments, and the ability to make agreements despite initially disadvantageous positions. The thinking of the anthropologist Gilberto Freyre was influential in the creation of Itamaraty's core doctrine. Freyre challenged negative assessments of Brazil's racially mixed society. He argued for Brazil to be considered a new and hybrid 'lusotropical' civilization that combined, in the Americas, the contributions of European, African, and indigenous civilizations. For Freyre, the Brazilian people were essentially generous, happy, sensual, peaceful, orderly, tolerant of racial and religious differences, and at peace with the world. Freyre also saw in the Baron of Rio Branco a representative of these values. While Freyre's ideas seem today to be based on racial stereotypes and a rather exaggerated belief in the harmony of Brazilian society, they gave Brazil's Foreign Ministry an attractive identity in the period of decolonization and civil rights after the Second World War.

For some, Itamaraty's core doctrine and high degree of professionalism make it a uniquely effective government ministry. The examination to enter Itamaraty is famously difficult, giving the ministry prestige. Itamaraty has overcome some of the deficiencies found in other parts of the Brazilian state and, in a boxing metaphor often used by diplomats, consistently 'punches above its weight'.

Brazil's ambiguous identity can also be seen as a key asset in its diplomacy. Brazil is a country that can claim to be both Western and non-Western, rich and poor, white and non-white, both a former colony and a former empire. Much of its population has European ancestry. Brazil's institutions look Western to European and North American eyes. On the other hand, roughly half of the population has some African ancestry. It also has a diverse and vibrant indigenous community. In the general population there are beliefs, practices, and customs that some would describe as non-Western, especially in the interior of the country and in indigenous reserves. Brazil's colonial history gives it affinities with the more recently decolonized countries of Africa and Asia. This furnishes Brazilian diplomats with a unique ability to dialogue with counterparts across the main dividing lines in global politics.

Brazil's foreign policy has been dualistic in that it has been based, at different times and places, on both the politics of prestige and the politics of a rules-based international order. The politics of prestige entails a claim for special privilege based on Brazil's unique status and characteristics. The politics of a rules-based international order is more universalistic, in that it defends the rights of smaller states in the international system to have their sovereignty respected and their voices heard, and for the rules of the global order to reflect their interests, experiences, and viewpoints. It is a defence of multipolarity, a broad sharing of powers between a number of influential states and a rejection of the dominance of a single or couple of states.

Brazil was the only Latin American country to send troops to fight in the Second World War. Brazil strengthened its military and became the most important industrial power in South America after the war, but its aspirations for international recognition were thwarted at the United Nations, created in 1945. Brazil pressed for but failed to win a permanent seat in the Security Council. Since that time, Brazil has continued to advocate a reform of the United Nations and its inclusion as a permanent member of the Security Council.

In Brazil's post-Second World War diplomacy, its relationship with the United States looms large as a major concern. This relationship is asymmetric: it is far more important to Brazil than it is to the United States. The brief and quixotic independent foreign policy of the Quadros (1961) and Goulart (1961–4) administrations set an important precedent that was later to become dominant in Itamaraty. Its core idea was that despite the bipolarity of the Cold War, developing countries had a right to pursue development and security on their own terms. The Non-Aligned Movement, established after the Bandung Conference in 1955, was also an expression of this desire. Brazil never formally joined the movement but it was an observer of the organization.

What all Brazilian governments have sought since redemocratization in the 1980s—before the arrival of the Bolsonaro administration in 2019—is some version of an independent foreign policy. To a lesser or greater degree, and with various political and ideological nuances, Brazilian foreign policy has sought autonomy and rejected automatic alignment with any single state. The sections that follow will look at Brazilian contributions to specific areas of global governance. In international development, sustainability, security, and health, Brazil has made constructive contributions to the rules-based international order.

International development

In the post-Second World War period Brazilian intellectuals made strong contributions to the critique of economic liberalism. Various Brazilian thinkers, including the economist Celso Furtado, started from the assumption that the policy recommendations of international financial institutions such as the International Monetary Fund and the World Bank are unlikely to consistently help a developing country such as Brazil because they reflect the experience and protect the interests of the rich countries of the global North. While differences between these thinkers existed, they all shared the view that Brazil had to pursue its own particular path to development, a path in which state institutions would coordinate and guide economic activity.

Brazil's gross domestic product per capita is close to the world average. It has characteristics of both an advanced capitalist and a developing country, making it suited to contributing to international debates about the management of the global economy. Brazil participated in the UN Economic Commission for Latin America (ECLAC), which recommended industrialization aimed at the domestic market insulated by high tariff walls. Brazil was also active in the establishment of the United Nations Conference on Trade and Development (UNCTAD), created in 1964 and headed by a Brazilian from 1995 to 2004. In the 1960s and 1970s, Brazil was active in the Group of 77 (G77), an association of developing countries founded at UNCTAD in 1964 which pushed for reforms of the global economic order. Brazil has a long lineage of intellectuals who have expressed a preoccupation with hunger, poverty, and economic inequality. The Recife-born geographer Josué de Castro, for example, gained worldwide recognition for his book *The Geography of Hunger*, a study of the global economic and political forces responsible for malnutrition that was published in English in 1952. De Castro served as president of the Council of the United Nations Food and Agricultural Organization (FAO) from 1952 to 1956.

With regard to world trade, Brazil was active in the Doha round of negotiations, launched in 2001. Brazil worked with other agro-exporting countries to push for liberalization of the agricultural markets of the European Union, Japan, and United States. In Cancun in 2003, Brazil partnered with India and China to make the case for a more equitable approach to liberalization in the Doha round. Although the result of the Cancun meeting was an impasse, and the Doha round petered out, in 2013 Brazil used its influence in the WTO to get its diplomat Roberto

Azevêdo elected director-general of that organization. Azevêdo was subsequently elected to a second mandate in 2017. During the Lula administration Brazilian foreign policy emphasized 'South–South' cooperation. This reflected the increase in trade between Brazil and partners in Asia (especially China), Africa, and the Middle East. Brazil expanded its diplomatic presence in and commercial exchange with Africa. It also became more involved in and integrated with its region of South America.

In recent years Brazil has expressed an interest in joining the Organization for Economic Development and Cooperation (OECD), the rich nations' club that already includes Mexico and Chile from Latin America and where Brazil is an observer. The thinking is that OECD membership would force Brazil to adhere to international best practices in economic regulation and thereby more tightly integrate Brazil into the global economy, enhancing its attractiveness to investors. This potential move is controversial. Some observers believe that OECD status is not worth it because Brazil would have to forgo developing country status in the WTO, a status that gives it certain advantages in that organization.

Sustainability

Brazil has played an important role in the global politics of climate change. In 1972 the Brazilian delegation to the United Nations Conference on the Human Environment in Stockholm took an anti-environmental stance, expressing the view that development and jobs had to come before conservation of nature. However, just a year later the Secretariat of the Environment was created in the Ministry of the Interior. Gradually a recognition that development and the environment are not antithetical took hold in the country. In 1983 the pioneering Brazilian environmentalist José Lutzenberger (1926–2002) published *The End of the Future? A Brazilian Ecological Manifesto* (*Fim do Futuro? Manifesto Ecológico Brasileiro*). In 1987 the politician and professor Paulo Nogueiro Neto represented Brazil in the

Brundtland Commission and contributed to its important report, published in 1987, *Our Common Future*. In 1989 IBAMA, the forest protection agency, was created.

Brazil's environmental movement is strong and as old as its counterparts in Europe and North America. Due to the movement the 1988 constitution has several ecological safeguards in place, including conservation areas, indigenous reserves, and the environmental licensing system. José Lutzenberger became minister of the environment in the Collor government (1990–2) and helped to organize the Eco 92 conference in Rio and demarcate the Yanomami reserve. In 1993 Brazil created the Ministry of the Environment, and in 2009, at the Copenhagen Climate Change Summit, pledged to reduce its CO_2 emissions by 36.1 to 38.9 per cent by 2020. In 2012 the Brazilian government passed a Forest Code. Despite its imperfections and compromises this legislation legally requires landowners in the Brazilian Amazon to maintain 80 per cent of their land as forest and facilitates the reforestation of denuded land. Brazilian participation was also important in the creation of the Paris Agreement on climate change in 2015.

The Amazon Fund was created by the Brazilian government in 2007 and is administered by the BNDES. The fund encourages sustainable livelihoods by supporting projects around the country and facilitating the enforcement of environmental laws. It is part of the United Nations' REDD programme (UN Collaborative Programme on Reducing Emissions from Deforestation and Forest Degradation in Developing Countries). The government of Norway contributed 93 per cent of the money disbursed by the Amazon Fund from 2008 to 2015, amounting to hundreds of millions of dollars, with the government of Germany and Petrobras picking up the rest. Norway's future contributions to the Fund are tied to Brazil maintaining rates of deforestation to specified limits. In addition, Brazilian agricultural producers know that if deforestation rates skyrocket, the European Union could use that fact to construct barriers to their exports.

When it comes to energy, Brazil has a record that is greener than that of most other nations. Roughly 45 per cent of its energy comes from renewables, including hydroelectric, ethanol, wind, and solar. Hydroelectric accounts for about 75 per cent of the electricity generated in the country. Nevertheless, hydroelectric is not free of negative social and environmental impacts. The Belo Monte Dam on the Xingu River in Pará, for example, completed in 2019, displaced thousands of people, including indigenous groups, which led to protests against it (see Figure 9). Because it has flooded large parts of jungle, it has also caused a loss of biodiversity and will produce large quantities of methane, a greenhouse gas. In addition, Brazil possesses large offshore deposits of oil in the so-called 'pre-salt' fields off the coast of Rio de Janeiro and São Paulo, and it remains to be seen how it will exploit this windfall.

9. A protest against the Belo Monte dam in Belém, Pará, August 2011.

Security

Brazil has been active in international peacekeeping operations. It has contributed some 50,000 troops to fifty different United Nations peacekeeping missions in the post-Second World War era. Its preference is for UN missions authorized under Chapter VI of the UN Charter, which requires agreement by the parties to a conflict and limits the ability of troops to engage, rather than missions authorized under Chapter VII, in which the United Nations can establish a peacekeeping operation without the consent of the parties to the conflict. From 1995 to 2002 Brazil was present in almost half of all United Nations peacekeeping operations. More recently, from 2004 to 2017 it headed the military component of MINUSTAH, the UN Mission to Haiti, and it also commanded the military operation of ONUMOZ in Mozambique in 1993–4, UNAVEM in Angola in 1989–91, and UNTAET in East Timor in 1999–2002. Brazil has also committed numerous civilians to UN peacekeeping missions including police personnel, election managers, judicial experts, human rights monitors, and economists. Brazil also has a peacekeeping training centre. The Joint Centre for Peace Operations in Brazil (CCOPAB) is named after Brazilian UN diplomat Sérgio Vieira de Mello (who was killed by a truck bomb in Baghdad in 2003) and located in Rio de Janeiro. In addition to training Brazilian peacekeepers it has trained military personnel from Argentina, Chile, France, Canada, and the USA.

Brazil was one of a small number of states that did not sign the Nuclear Nonproliferation Treaty in 1968. It objected to the inequality built into the NPT, which allows existing nuclear powers to keep their weapons while opposing the acquisition of the weapons by others. Brazil constructed a small domestic nuclear programme in the 1970s (two plants now contribute about 3 per cent of the country's overall energy) but chose not to develop a nuclear bomb even though it had the capability to do so. Working quietly with its neighbour Argentina, it made a pact that both nations would forgo the bomb, thus avoiding the tension that exists in other parts of the world, such as between India and Pakistan. It has a bilateral inspection regime with Argentina in the nuclear field. In 1998 Brazil finally signed the NPT, although not the additional protocol which allows for unannounced inspections of nuclear facilities. Brazil is a significant player in nuclear questions because it is one of the few countries to have capacity in all major dimensions of the nuclear fuel cycle, from mineral prospecting to the enrichment of uranium to the fabrication of nuclear fuel.

Global health

One of Brazil's most significant actions in global health occurred in the early 2000s when the HIV-AIDS crisis led to concern about infected people in developing countries. In 2001 approximately 100,000 AIDS patients in Brazil were taking antiretroviral drugs, thanks in part to a 1996 law that federalized the treatment of HIV-AIDS patients and offered antiretroviral drugs to those who needed them without charge. The then minister of health, José Serra, was worried about the cost of the medication. Aware that Brazilian companies had the capability to produce generic versions of the drugs, he invoked the health emergency clause of the Trade-Related Aspects of the Intellectual Property Rights (TRIPS) agreement of the World Health Organization (WHO) to threaten to break the patents of the big pharmaceutical companies. In May 2001 Serra said that he would allow a Brazilian firm to produce a generic version of Nelfinavir in July unless the Swiss company Roche lowered the price of the drug. This invocation of TRIPS led to agreements between the Brazilian government and some of the major pharmaceutical companies to lower their prices. At the WHO Serra defended the right of developing countries to gain access to the drugs for HIV-AIDS patients.

Religious nationalism

The Bolsonaro administration that came to power in 2019 broke from the foreign policies of the centre-right and centre-left governments that preceded it, at least rhetorically, because it had a different domestic political base and was built on a campaign in 2018 far to the right of any other winning campaign since 1989. Elements of the Bolsonaro perspective on foreign policy were close alignment with the Trump administration in the United States and the Netanyahu administration in Israel; support for other national populist governments in countries such as Hungary, Italy, and Poland; an aggressive condemnation of the Maduro regime in Venezuela; a sceptical view of climate change and a lukewarm, if not hostile attitude towards Brazil's voluntary commitments to reduce greenhouse gas emissions in the 2015 Paris Agreement; and a critical stance towards international norms in areas such as human rights and immigration.

The rise in the rate of deforestation in the first year of the Bolsonaro administration in 2019 created a backlash of criticism and concern that highlighted the novelty of the government's foreign policy. What was new was not so much the increase in the rate of deforestation itself, but the government's truculent attitude towards domestic environmentalists, NGOs, and foreign political leaders who raised concerns, and its apparent preference for predatory development over environmental conservation.

In May 2019 eight former ministers of the environment, including the former presidential candidate Marina Silva, wrote a letter criticizing the government's environmental policies. One of the signatories to the letter noted that although the Ministry of the Environment had been formally preserved, most of its primary functions had been transferred to other agencies. Another said that Brazil was violating its treaty obligations and had become a threat to the planet's climate. In August 2019 the governments of both Norway and Germany announced that they were suspending planned contributions to the Amazon Fund. This was due to the Bolsonaro government's unilateral abolition of the Amazon Fund's technical and steering committees, a move to diminish NGO participation in both bodies. This repudiation of the government's policies and attitudes by former ministers and foreign donors was unprecedented and showed how far Brazil had moved from the 'green games of Rio' in 2016.

The Bolsonaro administration shared many points of convergence with other national populist governments. For example, it was religious and enjoyed strong support from members of Pentecostal churches. Members of these churches, 70 per cent of whom voted for Bolsonaro, make up a quarter of the Brazilian electorate. When he took office in 2019, Foreign Minister Ernesto Araújo moved the Foreign Ministry's rhetoric in line with the pronouncements of the Bolsonaro administration. An ambassador who had never led an embassy abroad, Araújo was lifted from obscurity in 2018, partly on the basis of his 2017 article 'Trump and the West', which appeared in a journal of the Institute for International Relations Research, published by the Foreign Ministry.

The foreign minister is a religious nationalist who abhors the Enlightenment, the French Revolution, and cosmopolitanism. Unlike the nationalism of the Vargas era, which was largely secular, Araújo's nationalism embraces Christianity as a key component of Brazil's identity. He excoriates 'globalism', which he defines as anti-national and anti-traditional liberalism in social life and unfettered globalization in economic life. He subscribes to the world view of the US political scientist Samuel P. Huntington, who wrote of a 'clash of civilizations'. In Araújo's view, the West, of which Brazil is an integral part, has to rearm itself spiritually in order to confront not only external enemies, including radical Islam, but the 'enemy within', liberals and leftists who are supposedly sapping the West of its moral strength. In this so-called clash of civilizations Araújo comes down firmly on the side of the anti-immigrant, illiberal, nativist, and at times racist national populism of Europe and the United States. He embraces a conspiracy theory that claims that a global network of 'cultural Marxists' has infiltrated the media, universities, foundations, think tanks, and multilateral organizations to pursue its aim of world domination and the oppression of the individual, the free market, the family, and God through the use of insidious concepts such as human rights, climate change, social justice, racial and cultural diversity, and equality.

Religious nationalism threatens to undermine the pragmatic and constructive contributions of Brazilian foreign policy in various areas such as international development, sustainability, security, and health. This is in part because in aligning Brazil with one side in a 'clash of civilizations', the Bolsonaro administration risks putting Brazil in harm's way in international conflicts involving religion, and diminishes Brazil's role as a respected interlocutor around the world. Domestically, it risks alienating not only the small numbers of atheists and other non-Christians in Brazil, but also the greater number of religious citizens who do not want their country to abandon its secular tradition in international relations, which has endured since the founding of the republic.

Many of the changes initially announced by the Bolsonaro administration were not carried out because of the weight of the economic interests against them. For example, the idea of moving the Brazilian Embassy from Tel Aviv to Jerusalem, in imitation of the Trump administration and floated as a possibility by President Bolsonaro, was downgraded to the opening of a commercial office in Jerusalem instead. Brazilian agribusiness companies that export halal meat to the Arab Middle East were a factor in this outcome. Brazil's withdrawal from the 2015 Paris Agreement on climate change, also at one point mooted by the president, was avoided in part because of the vulnerability of Brazilian agro-exporters to Europe to possible sanctions for environmental reasons. In a similar fashion, President Bolsonaro's anti-China rhetoric on the campaign trail was replaced by a more moderate stance in power. Unlike the United States Brazil has a trade surplus with China. Although that trade is unbalanced, with Brazil largely exporting commodities and importing manufactured goods, China is a larger trading partner than the United States for Brazil. It is also a major investor, including in oil and gas exploration, electricity, and other infrastructure projects. Under such circumstances any Brazilian government has a strong incentive to protect and nurture that relationship.

The future of Brazil's foreign policy

Brazil does not project military force abroad in an offensive fashion. It prefers to build up its military capability for defensive purposes, in order to guard the fresh water and biodiversity of the Amazon basin and the offshore oil deposits along its South Atlantic coast. Because of its distinctive profile, Brazil's global influence depends—to a much greater extent than regional military powers such as China, India, and Russia—on the perceived attractiveness of its economic and political model. When that model appears to be successful, as it did during the period of stability and consensus of 1995–2010, Brazil's visibility and influence rise significantly. But when Brazil appears to be politically polarized and in the grip of an illiberal populist nationalist government, as it has recently, then its influence tends to wane.

For the best part of sixty years, Brazilian foreign policy has emphasized autonomy, multipolarity, peace, negotiation, international law, and pragmatism. It has been an advocate of moderate reform of the institutions of global governance and a critic of the unilateralism of the great powers. Born in the Cold War, this posture acquired universal significance because it implicitly criticized the way that the superpower rivalry between the USSR and USA reduced developing countries to client states. In the post-Cold War era, the Brazilian emphasis on multipolarity resonated with the views of other emerging powers and developing countries.

Brazil has made an impact in several policy areas, including international development, sustainability, security, and global health. In the 2000s it became more influential and visible in some of those areas, and it prioritized its membership in some key regional and global organizations, including its trade bloc Mercosur, the BRICS group, and the financial G20. Brazil's activism on the environment led to the Rio 92 conference and a series of negotiations that culminated in the 2015 Paris Agreement on climate change. Brazil's success in reducing poverty in the 2000s contributed to the selection of no poverty and zero hunger as the first and second goals respectively of the United Nations' Sustainable Development Goals.

The inaugural address of Brazil's foreign minister in 2019 marks a deviation from Brazil's foreign policy tradition. Instead of autonomy, Brazil has sought alignment with the Trump administration of the United States. Instead of cooperative multipolarity, Brazil has sided with critics of 'globalism' and the 'global agenda', propagators of an aggressive national populism that sees much of the international agenda, including the consensus on respect for human rights and commitments to deal with climate change, as unacceptable constraints on national sovereignty. The latter is particularly alarming given Brazil's control over almost two-thirds of the Amazon rainforest, which plays such a pivotal role in mitigating the effects of greenhouse gas emissions.

Instead of secularism and tolerance, Brazilian foreign policy appears to be based on a theocratic approach to world politics and alarmist theories about threats to the Christian West. Perhaps even more baffling given Brazil's racially mixed population, the foreign minister praised leaders who use ethno-nationalist and racist tropes to mobilize their base. It is not surprising, therefore, that observers of Brazilian foreign policy are confused. It remains to be seen whether that moment in the Foreign Ministry in 2019 represents a temporary deviation from the status quo or a critical juncture in the trajectory of Brazil's international relations. If it is the latter, the world would lose an important voice for reason at a time when it desperately needs one. And Brazil, with its modest military capability, could fare badly if the trend towards illiberal and belligerent nationalism spirals into international conflict.

Chapter 8
Exuberance and diversity

On Saturday 25 May 2019 the Park of the City in Brasília, Brazil's capital, was a busy place. Underneath a glorious blue sky and amidst bright sunshine—it was 31 degrees Celsius—the 420 hectares of the park thronged with activity. The lively scenes in the park, the official name of which is the Sarah Kubitschek Park, in honour of the former first lady and wife of the founder of the city, President Juscelino Kubitschek, were very unlike the civic ritual described at the beginning of this book, the opening ceremony of the Olympic Games in 2016. Unlike the latter, the hustle and bustle of the park—which is bigger than Central Park in New York City—was not something planned and executed by state authorities, nor was it meant to showcase Brazil to the outside world. It was instead the spontaneous and uncoordinated expression of the leisure-time interests of residents of the city (see Figure 10). Brazilians of all shapes, sizes, ages, colours, orientations, and dispositions shared the beautiful public space harmoniously. The state was present but it was not repressive. Inequalities were visible but they were not excessive.

At the entrance to the park, the military police were celebrating the 210th anniversary of their founding with an exhibition of vehicles and equipment. A military police helicopter was in the parking lot, with a long line of people waiting to sit in the cockpit. A phalanx of parked police motorcycles attracted large numbers of

10. Parque da Cidade Dona Sarah Kubitschek in the Asa Sul part of Brasília.

people, as did buses and patrol cars. Children rode pedal carts around a track, and a military police band cranked out well-known rock music hits. Three officers on horseback moved around the area, while under canopies information about the military police was available to curious passers-by. There were many uniformed police officers present, but they were in the park less to provide security and more to celebrate the history of their organization and engage in public relations with residents of the city.

Many had come to the park to exercise. On the asphalt trails, runners shared the space with cyclists, roller bladers, people on scooters, skate boarders, and walkers. On the grass alongside the trails, boys kicked soccer balls, perhaps dreaming of becoming the next Neymar, the Brazilian football star who once played for Santos, the same club as Pelé. Tennis courts were filled with the echoes of serves and volleys, while sunburned veterans of paddle ball (frescobol) stood on sand dressed in miniature swimsuits while whacking the ball at each other. In one section of the park two boys threw an American football at each other, while body

119

sculptors used equipment scattered throughout the park to do sit-ups, pull-ups, resistance exercises, and stretches.

In the pines in the south-western edge of the park families crowded around picnic tables while smoke from barbecue pits curled up towards the blue sky, the high rolling plateau of the cerrado behind them in the distance. The smell of barbecued meat wafted through the air.

Some members of these families lounged in hammocks strung between trees. Couples canoodled on blankets in the shade. Children ran exuberantly amongst the trees while babies were cuddled and cradled by mothers, fathers, aunts, uncles, and grandparents. A man and his son manipulated a drone that was rising and falling in the air above them.

Some in the park were more interested in rest, relaxation, and food than exercise. They were faced with a lot of choice. In addition to stalls and snack bars, the park was full of mobile vendors who still needed to work despite it being a weekend. They offered the public cotton candy, crisps, the purple Amazonian fruit *açaí* (usually eaten as a frozen concentrate, a bit like ice cream), *churros* (sweet fried dough pastries), and *pasteis* (fried stuffed pastries). A variety of drinks were available, including coconut water, sugarcane juice, water, and beer. In shady clusters throughout the park, groups of people sat and took in the scene while eating, drinking, and conversing.

Music filled the air. On one part of the trail in the middle of the park, a couple practised dance moves to the sound of music coming from a small black sound system placed on the ground. In several parts of the park stages were filled by bands playing a variety of different types of music. Elsewhere recorded music and radios accompanied people in their varied activities. In the north-eastern edge of the park in a section named after Ana Lídia, a 7-year-old girl who was kidnapped and killed in 1973 and whose killer was never found, the Nova Nicolândia fun fair was in full swing. Children screamed on the most anxiety-inducing rides, while a large ferris wheel rotated serenely in the middle of the fair.

Brazil's promise

The Park of the City in Brasília on this bright day in May reflected the dazzling exuberance, energy, joy, and diversity of Brazil. It also offered an implicit response to some of the questions about the country raised at the beginning of this book. If doubts exist as to whether Brazil can preserve its environment, be a country better than its origins, innovate and contribute to science, become less violent and more inclusive, and remain globally influential, then the park on that day seemed to offer hope that it can. In the Park of the City, everyone seemed to be fully exercising her or his capabilities. The green space was a public good that ameliorated inequalities and provided a foundation for active citizenship. Everyone could enjoy it, and everyone kept out of each other's way, tolerating and accepting difference. Why can't Brazil become more equal, more just, more efficient, less violent, more developed, and more globally influential than the country that exists at present?

We have seen in this book that although Brazil has half a millennium of history, the idea of Brazil is relatively new, and the consolidation of the country into a fixed territory with a strong central state and a common identity for its people was an accomplishment of the early 20th century. That century was one of wrenching change, involving profound transformations from an agrarian to an urban country, the centralization of state power, and national integration. The country also experienced two dictatorships in the 20th century, under the New State of Getúlio Vargas from 1937 to 1945 and the period of military rule from 1964 to 1985.

In the face of the innumerable challenges of the 21st century, it is useful to remind ourselves of the obstacles that Brazil successfully overcame in the 20th. Brazil escaped the vulnerabilities of being overly dependent on a single agricultural commodity, coffee, in a volatile world economy. It industrialized after 1930, achieving high levels of growth between 1930 and 1980, becoming the largest economy in Latin America and one of the ten largest economies in the world. In the 1980s the country joined a global wave of democratization, ending a twenty-one-year dictatorship and promulgating a new constitution. In a period of stability between 1995 and 2010, it embarked on a number of innovative experiments in democratic participation and economic inclusion, reducing poverty and even some income inequality in the process. And in the post-Second World War period Brazil found a distinctive voice in world affairs with a foreign policy that was pragmatic, moderate, and multipolar, a bridge between North and South, developed and developing, Western and non-Western.

New challenges

Success breeds new challenges. Despite Brazil's industrialization, some of that industry now appears to be uncompetitive. The country seems to be caught in a low-growth trap and is searching for a new model that can allow the economy to innovate and move up the value-added chain into more technologically advanced forms of production. Solving the growth dilemma is crucial, because only with growth can poverty be further reduced and inequalities lessened. In terms of democracy, the crisis of representation and the deeply polarized electorate make governance difficult. Active citizenship could offer a way out of this impasse, as people make their voices heard and demand accountability and transparency from their elected officials. In foreign policy, state managers have flirted with a religious nationalist ideology that is a repudiation of Brazil's diplomatic past and a threat to many of the country's material interests. But Brazil's credibility and influence can be restored if it reclaims the professionalism and pragmatism of its diplomatic tradition.

11. The Amazon rainforest as seen from above.

Brazil remains a country of contradictions. For example, it has the second-largest forest cover of all the countries in the world (after Russia) but in most years it also deforests a larger area than any other country (see Figure 11). It is a country of race mixture and the notion of racial democracy, but racial inequality is evident in many aspects of its society, including the criminal justice system, schools, and the labour market. In its external relations it is pacific, but its rates of internal violence are high. It is the fourth largest democracy in the world, but in 2018 it elected a president who praises Brazil's military dictatorship of 1964–85. These and other contradictions mark Brazil as complex, as well as large and rapidly changing. As the composer Tom Jobim once said, Brazil is not for beginners.

Some Brazilians have given up on Brazil, joining the diaspora abroad and rejecting the promise of a better country as a fiction. But the majority have not. Everyone should want Brazil to succeed as a nation, to overcome the obstacles to its economic development, to resolve its crisis of representation and strengthen its democracy, maintain its diplomatic traditions, and achieve peace, justice, and dignity for its citizens. That is because Brazil occupies a pivotal position in the world, halfway between the affluent and poor nations, and has an ability to dialogue with both the Global North and the Global South, both the 'West' and the rest. The problems Brazil faces—inequality, poverty, violence, environmental degradation, political polarization, pandemics, and a gap between the populace and its representatives—are the world's problems. Brazil: we've all been there. Brazil is the world and the world is Brazil.

Timeline

18,000–38,000 BC	Asian peoples walk across the Bering Strait and/or travel by boat to South America and occupy what is now Brazil.
7 June 1494	The Treaty of Tordesillas, dividing the New World between Portugal and Spain, is signed.
24 April 1500	A Portuguese fleet commanded by Pedro Álvares Cabral lands on the north-east coast of South America at what is now Porto Seguro, Bahia, Brazil.
1530	The trade in African slaves to Brazil begins. From then until the mid-19th century an estimated 4 to 5 million African slaves are shipped to Brazil.
20 November 1695	Zumbi, the leader of the Palmares settlement, is killed by Portuguese troops.
1695	Portuguese colonists discover gold in what is now the state of Minas Gerais, Brazil.
21 April 1792	Joaquim José da Silva Xavier, a dentist known as Tiradentes (toothpuller), is executed for his part in a conspiracy to overthrow Portuguese rule in Brazil.

8 March 1808	King João VI and the Portuguese court, numbering some 10,000–15,000 people, arrive in Rio de Janeiro, in a fleet escorted by the British Navy.
25 April 1821	King João VI returns to Portugal, leaving his son, King Pedro I, as regent.
7 September 1822	Pedro I declares independence from Portugal, creating the Brazilian Empire.
23 November 1826	Great Britain and Brazil sign a treaty formally ending the slave trade to Brazil.
7 April 1831	Dom Pedro II becomes emperor of Brazil.
December 1864	The Paraguay War between Paraguay on one side and Argentina, Brazil, and Uruguay on the other, begins. It ends on 1 March 1870.
5 October 1897	Brazilian troops overcome the last defenders of Canudos, a community in north-east Brazil led by Antônio the Counsellor.
13 May 1888	Slavery is abolished in the Golden Law and an estimated 600,000 slaves are freed.
15 November 1889	The army, led by Marshal Manuel Deodoro da Fonseca, proclaims the beginning of a republic, and Dom Pedro II is sent into exile.
11–18 February 1922	Modern Art Week, a celebration of artistic and literary modernism, is held in São Paulo.
25 March 1922	The Brazilian Communist Party (PCB) is founded.
3 October 1930	The Liberal Alliance, a coalition that had lost the presidential election five months before and led by Getúlio Vargas, stages a successful revolt against the government.
12 October 1931	The Christ the Redeemer statue is inaugurated in Rio de Janeiro.

9 July 1932	An armed uprising against the government breaks out in São Paulo. On 2 October loyalist troops occupy São Paulo and depose the rebel government.
1 December 1933	*The Masters and the Slaves (Casa Grande e Senzala)* by Gilberto Freyre is published.
23–7 November 1935	A Communist uprising that includes junior officers and enlisted men in the navy and army occurs in Natal, Recife, and Rio and is crushed by the government.
10 November 1937	President Vargas carries out an auto-coup, promulgates a new, authoritarian constitution, and declares the creation of a New State that endures until 1945.
30 June 1944	The first contingent of the Brazilian Expeditionary Force of 25,000 troops leaves Brazil for Italy to fight for the Allies in the Second World War under US command.
29 October 1945	Getúlio Vargas is eased out of the presidency in a coup. General Eurico Gaspar Dutra, Vargas's minister of war, runs for and wins the presidency on 2 December.
3 October 1950	Getúlio Vargas wins the election, becoming president in 1951.
24 August 1954	President Getúlio Vargas commits suicide.
29 June 1958	Brazil wins the FIFA World Cup for the first time, beating Sweden 5–2 in the final in Stockholm, with the 17-year-old Pelé scoring two goals.
21 April 1960	Brasília, Brazil's new capital, is inaugurated.
25 August 1961	President Jânio Quadros resigns, triggering a political crisis that is eventually resolved with the ascension to the presidency of Vice-President João Goulart.

31 March 1964	A military–civilian coalition initiates a self-proclaimed revolution and deposes President João Goulart.
13 December 1968	The authoritarian regime temporarily closes Congress and issues the Fifth Institutional Act (AI-5), which gives the executive sweeping new powers.
29 August 1974	President Ernesto Geisel announces a political relaxation (*distenção*).
13 March 1979	Auto workers led by the union leader Luiz Inácio 'Lula' da Silva go on strike in the industrial suburbs of São Paulo Santo André, São Bernardo do Campo, and São Caetano do Sul.
28 August 1979	The authoritarian regime issues an amnesty, freeing most political prisoners, allowing the return of political exiles, and absolving members of the security forces of responsibility for human rights violations.
10 February 1980	The Workers' Party (Partido dos Trabalhadores) is founded.
15 March 1985	José Sarney is sworn in as the first civilian president since 1964.
27 February 1994	The Plano Real begins. In a series of measures it reduces inflation and helps the presidential candidacy of the finance minister, Fernando Henrique Cardoso.
5 October 1988	The new constitution, approved by Congress on 22 September, comes into effect.
13–14 June 1992	Brazil hosts Eco-92 or the Rio de Janeiro Earth Summit, a major United Nations conference focused on sustainability.
29 December 1992	President Fernando Collor de Mello is impeached and replaced by his vice-president, Itamar Franco.

3 October 1994	Fernando Henrique Cardoso is elected president, eventually serving two terms.
27 October 2002	Lula is elected president, serving two consecutive terms.
30 April 2004	MINUSTAH, the UN peacekeeping operation in Haiti, is established, with Brazil leading the military part of the operation.
20 June 2013	An estimated 2 million people protest in over 400 cities during the Confederations Cup, a warm-up for the 2014 World Cup.
17 March 2014	The Carwash (*Lava Jato*) anti-corruption investigation begins when a Federal Police inquiry into the activities of money launderer Alberto Youssef uncovers a kickback scheme in the partially state-owned oil company Petrobras.
10 December 2014	The Truth Commission publishes its report on human rights abuses of the authoritarian regime of 1964–85 after more than two years of work.
5 August 2016	The opening ceremony of the Rio Olympic Games occurs in Maracanã stadium.
31 August 2016	President Dilma Rousseff is impeached in the Senate and replaced by her vice-president, Michel Temer.
14 July 2017	Federal Judge Sérgio Moro convicts former President Lula and sentences him to nine years and six months for bribe taking and money laundering.
26 June 2017	Prosecutor General Rodrigo Janot charges President Michel Temer in the Supreme Court with bribe taking.
14 March 2018	Marielle Franco, a Rio councilwoman from the Socialism and Liberty Party (PSOL) and critic of the police and *milícias* (criminal groups linked to the police), is assassinated together with her driver in downtown Rio de Janeiro.

7 April 2018	Lula turns himself in to the Federal Police in Curitiba, Paraná, to begin his sentence.
27 October 2018	Jair Bolsonaro wins the presidency.
8 November 2019	Lula is released from jail due to a Supreme Court ruling that defendants cannot be imprisoned until all their appeals have been exhausted.
16 April 2020	President Bolsonaro, minimizing the threat of the coronavirus pandemic and opposing social isolation measures in states and municipalities, fires his Health Minister Luiz Henrique Mandetta.

References

Chapter 1: Brazil hosts the Olympic Games

Brazil's territorial ranking is from Worldometers: <https://www.worldometers.info/world-population/brazil-population/>. The population is from the Brazilian Institute of Geography and Statistics (IBGE) at <https://www.ibge.gov.br/apps/populacao/projecao//>. The relative size of the economy is from the World Bank <https://databank.worldbank.org/data/download/GDP_PPP.pdf>.The figure of 50,000 plant species in the Amazon basin is from the Yale School of Forestry and Environmental Studies, Global Forest Atlas, at <https://globalforestatlas.yale.edu/amazon/ecoregions/ecology-amazon-rainforest>.

The figure that almost two-thirds of the Amazon rainforest is in Brazil comes from Fabíola Ortiz, 'Ten years on, Amazon Fund receives applause, criticism, faces new tests', in *Mongabay*, 21 December 2018, at <https://news.mongabay.com/2018/12/ten-years-on-amazon-fund-receives-applause-criticism-faces-new-tests/>.

The plan to plant 24 million trees for the Rio Olympics, and how the plan was not fulfilled, is described in Carol Knoploch, 'Floresta dos Atletas aina são mudas e estão guardadas em viveiro no Rio' in *O Globo*, 19 August 2018, at <https://oglobo.globo.com/esportes/floresta-dos-atletas-ainda-sao-mudas-estao-guardadas-em-viveiro-no-rio-22987401 on 23 July 2019>.

The figure of almost 20 per cent of the Amazon rainforest in Brazil being destroyed is from the climate scientist Antonio Donato Nobre in Camilla Costa, '"A grande mentira verde": como a destruição da Amazônia vai além do desmatamento', 13 February 2020, at *BBC*

Brasil <https://www.bbc.com/portuguese/brasil-51317040>. (Donato Nobre believes that if degradation and not just deforestation is taken into account, the figure is higher than 20 per cent.) The decline in the rate of deforestation in the Brazilian Amazon between 2004 and 2012 is Prodes data at the website of Brazil's National Institute for Space Research (INPE), at <http://terrabrasilis.dpi.inpe.br/app/dashboard/deforestation/biomes/legal_amazon/rates>. The increase between 2018 and 2019 is from the same source.

The projection about the tipping point for the Amazon rainforest is from Thomas E. Lovejoy and Carlos Nobrega, 'Editorial: Amazon Tipping Point', *Science Advances*, Volume 4, Number 2, 21 February 2018, at <https://advances.sciencemag.org/content/4/2/eaat2340>.

Jessé Souza, *A elite do atraso: da escravidão à Lava Jato* (Rio de Janeiro: Leya, 2017).

Some of the information on Santos Dumont is from 'Highlights in Aviation: Alberto Santos-Dumont, Brazil', Smithsonian Education, at <http://www.smithsonianeducation.org/scitech/impacto/graphic/aviation/alberto.html>.

The estimate of the number of indigenous people in Brazil comes from E. Bradford Burns, *A History of Brazil* (New York: Columbia University Press, third edition, 1993), p. 15.

IBGE reported the indigenous population in the 2010 census as 817,900, with indigenous reserves accounting for 12.5 per cent of the national territory. From 'IBGE divulga resultado do censo 2010 sobre população indígena', in *FUNAI Notícias* 10 August 2012, at <http://www.funai.gov.br/index.php/comunicacao/noticias/1757-ibge-divulga-resultado-do-censo-2010-sobre-populacao-indigena?start=1>. The information on indigenous groups and languages is from the same source.

About the dancers from Amazonia portraying indigenous people in the opening ceremony of the Olympic games, I am grateful to the anthropologist Betty Mindlin. Personal communication from Betty Mindlin, 2 February 2019.

The information on the forcible relocation of families prior to the Rio Olympics is from Letícia Osório, who uses an estimate of 22,059 families, in '2016 Olympic Games: What Rio doesn't want the world to see', in *Equals Change Blog*, Ford Foundation, 4 August 2016, at <https://www.fordfoundation.org/ideas/equals-change-blog/posts/2016-olympic-games-what-rio-doesn-t-want-the-world-to-see/>.

The information on the total number of killings in Brazil and the number of killings by the police comes from the Brazilian Forum for Public Security, Public Security in Numbers 2019, at <http://www.forumseguranca.org.br/wpcontent/uploads/2019/02/Infografico_an12_atualizado.pdf>.

The information on the arrest of Nuzman is from 'Carlos Arthur Nuzman é preso por suspeita de fraude na escolha do Rio 2016', *Forum*, 5 October 2017, at <https://revistaforum.com.br/carlos-arthur-nuzman-e-preso-por-suspeita-de-fraude-na-escolha-da-rio-2016/>. The information on Cabral comes from Rafa Santos, 'Cabral recebe nova condenação e penas já somam 280 anos', *Consultor Jurídico*, 29 January 2020, at <https://www.conjur.com.br/2020-jan-29/cabral-condenado-14-anos-penas-somam-280-anos>.

Chapter 2: From colony to empire to republic

The incident concerning Charles Darwin comes from chapter 2, Rio de Janeiro, in *The Voyage of the Beagle: A Naturalist's Voyage Round the World*, found at <https://www.coolgalapagos.com/Darwin_voyage_beagle/darwin_beagle_chapter_2.php>.

Jean de Léry, *History of a Voyage to the Land of Brazil* (Berkeley: University of California Press, 1993).

Maria Fernandes Rodrigues, 'Reencontro com os origens: Daniel Munduruku faz ponte entre suas duas culturas em livro de crônicas', *O Estado de São Paulo* 6 April 2019, p. C3 for the figure of 60,000 indigenous students in Brazilian universities and André Barracal, 'Guerra às Universidades', *Carta Capital* 8 May 2019, pp. 18–25 (the figure on p. 21 gives the total number of students in Brazilian universities).

On European seaborne empires see Jason Sharman, *Empires of the Weak: The Real Story of European Expansion and the Creation of the New World Order* (Princeton: Princeton University Press, 2019).

The estimate of 4 million Africans and other information in this paragraph comes from Marshall Eakin, *Brazil: The Once and Future Country* (New York: Palgrave Macmillan, 1998), p. 18; and Boris Fausto and Sergio Fausto, *A Concise History of Brazil* (New York: Cambridge University Press, second edition, 2014), p. 18.

The information that Brazil had the largest slave population in the world, roughly 50 per cent of its population of 3 million people, comes from Marshall Eakin (1998), p. 115.

The information on the percentage of Afro-Brazilians in the four largest provinces at the end of the colonial period and the percentage of the non-white free population comes from Boris Fausto and Sergio Fausto (2014), p. 26.

The figure of 600,000 Portuguese coming to Brazil from 1700 to 1760 comes from Boris Fausto and Sergio Fausto (2014), p. 49.

Sérgio Buarquede Holanda, *Roots of Brazil* (South Bend, Ind.: University of Notre Dame Press, 2012).

Roberto Schwarz, 'Misplaced Ideas: Literature and Society in Late Nineteenth-Century Brazil', *Comparative Civilizations Review* Volume 5, Number 5, 1980, Article 3, at <https://scholarsarchive. byu.edu/cgi/viewcontent.cgi?article=1030&context=ccr>.

The estimate of 10,000 to 15,000 coming to Rio with the court comes from Boris Fausto and Sergio Fausto (2014), p. 64.

The estimate of 300,000 deaths in the Paraguay War comes from Rubens Ricupero, *A diplomacia na construção do Brasil 1750–2016* (São Paulo: Versal, 2017), p. 209.

The information about the naval rebellion in 1893–4 comes from Rubens Ricupero (2017), p. 265.

The total number of immigrants between 1890 and 1930 is estimated at 3,800,000, or 22 per cent of the 17 million Brazilians counted in the 1900 census. This comes from Rubens Ricupero (2017), p. 257.

The quote about the province of São Paulo comes from Ulick Ralph Burke and Robert Staples Jr, *Business and Pleasure in Brazil* (London: Field and Tuer, Ye Leadenhall Presse SC and New York: Scribner and Welford, 1886), p. 140.

Chapter 3: The Vargas era and its legacy

The information about Vargas's development of political skills comes from Lira Neto, *Getúlio: 1882-1930: dos anos de formaçã à conquista do poder* (São Paulo: Companhia das Letras, 2012), pp. 28–57; 174–93; 272–98.

The discussion of interventores comes from Laurence Whitehead, 'State Organization in Latin America since 1930', in Leslie Bethell, ed., *The Cambridge History of Latin America: 1930 to the Present*, Volume VI, Part 2 (Cambridge: Cambridge University Press, 2008), pp. 1–96, pp. 21–2.

Getulio Vargas said in Petrópolis in 1937, 'The Armed Forces will never permit other flags to wave higher than ours'. From Lira Neto, *Getúlio: 1930–1945: do governo provisório à ditadura do Estado Novo* (São Paulo: Companhia das Letras, 2013), p. 289.

The burning of the twenty state flags is from Laurence Whitehead (2008), p. 22.

Daryle Williams, *Culture Wars in Brazil: The First Vargas Regime, 1930–1945* (Durham, NC: Duke University Press, 2001).

The detail about Vargas's comment to Valdemar Ferreira comes from Lira Neto (2013), p. 289. The quote is: 'My proposal is the maintenance of order, because I do not want what occurred in '32 with the Paulista Revolution to happen again.'

The claim that critics thought the São Paulo Força Pública was excessively militarized comes from Samira Bueno Nunes, *Bandido Bom é Bandido Morto: A opção ideológico-institucional da política de segurança pública na manutenção de padrões de atuação violentos da polícia militar paulista* (São Paulo: MA Thesis, Escola de Administração de Empresas de São Paulo, FGV, 2014), p. 41.

The information on ISEB comes from Ronald H. Chilcote, *Intellectuals and the Search for National Identity in Twentieth-Century Brazil* (New York: Cambridge University Press, 2014), pp. 57–101.

On the Brazilian victory in the 1958 World Cup final see Nelson Rodrigues, *À sombra das chuteiras imortais: crônicas de futebol* (São Paulo: Companhia das Letras, 1993), pp. 51–2 and 60–1.

Chapter 4: Dictatorship and repression

On operation Brother Sam, see Phyllis Parker, *Brazil and the Quiet Intervention, 1964* (Austin: University of Texas Press, 1979).

On the figures of those killed under the various dictatorships, see Argentine National Commission on the Disappeared, *Nunca Más* (London: Faber and Faber, 1986); José Zalaquett, *Report of the Chilean National Commission on Truth and Reconciliation* (South Bend, Ind.: University of Notre Dame Press, 1993), Volumes I and II; Comissão Nacional da Verdade, *Relatório da Comissão Nacional da Verdade* (2014), Volumes I–III, at <http://cnv.memoriasreveladas.gov.br/>.

About the pro-coup video released by the president's office, see Hanrrikson de Andrade, 'Funcionário achou que vídeo pró-golpe

era da Previdência, diz ministro' in *BOL Notícias*, 13 June 2019, at
<https://www.bol.uol.com.br/noticias/2019/06/13/funcionario-achou-que-video-pro-golpe-era-da-previdencia-diz-ministro.htm>.

Chapter 5: Rich country, poor people: economic challenges

The description of the rural trade union in Itambé is based on field
notes by the author, who conducted research on the rural trade
unions of the sugar zone of Pernambuco in 1988.

The comparison between industrial output in Brazil and Japan
between 1965 and 1980 is from Vinicius Rodrigues Vieira,
'Blended Diplomacy: Institutional Design and Brazil's National
Interest in Trade', *Rising Powers Quarterly*, Volume 2, Issue 2,
2017, pp. 31–53, reference on p. 35.

Data on growth rates are from Matthew Taylor, *Decadent
Developmentalism: The Political Economy of Democratic Brazil*
(Cambridge: Cambridge University Press, forthcoming),
chapter 1, pp. 6–7.

Data on declining inequality in Brazil, Chile, and Peru come from
Matthew Taylor (forthcoming), chapter 1, p. 8.

Data on the acquisition of public land come from Sérgio Leite,
'Políticas públicas e agricultura no Brasil: comentários sobre o
cenário recente', in Ivo Lesbaupin, ed., *O desmonte da nação:
balanço do governo FHC* (Petrópolis: Editora Vozes, 1998),
pp. 153–80; the reference is to p. 173.

On deindustrialization, the data on the decline of manufacturing in
the economy and the share of manufacturing in exports come from
'Desindustrialização no Brasil é real e estrutural', in Centro de
Estudos do Desenvolvimento Econômico (CEDE), at <https://
www3.eco.unicamp.br/cede/centro/146-destaque/508-
desindustrializacao-no-brasil-e-real-e-estrutural>.

On Brumadinho see Joana Oliveira, 'Festival em Brumadinho marca
linha tênue entre a cura e o reforço da dor do luto na cidade', in *El
País*, 20 May 2019, at <www.brasil.elpais.com>.

The data on Bolsa Família and the CadÚnico come from Tereza
Campello and Marcelo Cortês Neri, eds, *Programa Bolsa Família:
Uma década de inclusão e cidadania—sumário executivo* (Brasília:
IPEA, 2014), pp. 9, 14–15, 18, and 31–2. All conversions from the
Brazilian currency, the real, to US dollars in this and other
passages in the book use the rate of R$4.39375 per dollar that
existed on 21 February 2020.

The figure on total social spending comes from Alfred Montero,
   Brazil: Reversal of Fortune (Cambridge: Polity Press, 2014), p. 139.
The data on inclusive growth come from Tereza Campello and Marcelo
   Cortês Neri (2014), p. 29; and Alfred Montero (2014), p. 133.
The information on the decline of inequality comes from Ricardo
   Barros, Samuel Franco, Mirela de Carvalho, and Rosane Mendonça,
   'Markets, the State and the Dynamics of Inequality in Brazil', in
   Luis F. López-Calva and Nora Lustig, eds, *Declining Inequality in
   Latin America: A Decade of Progress?* (New York/Washington DC:
   Brookings Institution Press, 2010), pp. 134–74; the reference is
   to p. 137.
The data on the increase in the percentage of people in poverty in
   Brazil between 2014 and 2017 come from 'Poverty Headcount
   Ratio at $5.50 a day (2011 PPP) (% of population)', in World Bank
   Data, <https://data.worldbank.org/indicator/SI.POV.
   UMIC?locations=BR>.
The data on the unemployment and growth rates come from *The
   Economist*, Volume 435, Number 9193, 9–15 May 2020 (Economic
   and financial indicators), p. 74.
The budget figure comes from 'União tem 93% de gastos obrigatórios',
   Epoca Negócios, 29 March 2018, at <https://epocanegocios.globo.
   com/Economia/noticia/2018/03/epoca-negocios-uniao-tem-93-
   de-gastos-obrigatorios.html>. See also 'Bolsa Família, Brazil's
   admired anti-poverty programme, is flailing', *The Economist*, 30
   January 2020 at <http://www.economist.com>.
Brazil's tax revenues averaged almost 34 per cent of GDP in the first
   part of the 2010s. This is from Gabriel Ondetti, 'The Roots of
   Brazil's Heavy Taxation', *Journal of Latin American Studies*,
   Volume 47, July 2015, pp. 749–79, citation on p. 749.
The data on savings rates come from Matthew Taylor (forthcoming),
   chapter 1, p. 7.
The data on the 2007 IBOPE poll and the 2018 survey on the
   privatization of Petrobras come from Matthew Taylor
   (forthcoming), chapter 3, p. 21. The data on the survey on the
   government being responsible for generating prosperity come
   from the same source, p. 22.
The data of 17 million Brazilians in 1900 come from Rubens Ricupero
   (2017), p. 257.
The data on birth rates in Brazil and the world average come from
   James Gallagher, 'Quase metade dos países tem nascimentos
   insuficientes para evitar declínio da população', 9 November 2018

at BBC Brasil, <https://www.bbc.com/portuguese/geral-46149577> and IBGE at <https://cidades.ibge.gov.br/brasil/panorama>.

The projection of Brazil's mid-21st-century population comes from Carlos Brito and Darlan Alvarenga, 'População brasileira chegará a 233 milhoes em 2047 e começerá a encolher, aponta IBGE', on 25 July 2018, at *Globo.com*, at <https://g1.globo.com/economia/noticia/2018/07/25/populacao-brasileira-chegara-a-233-milhoes-em-2047-e-comecara-a-encolher-aponta-ibge.ghtml>.

Chapter 6: Democratic development or decay?

On the percentage of women in Congress, see Beatriz Motesanti, 'Mulheres são 15% do novo Congresso, mas índice ainda é baixo', in *UOL*, 8 October 2018, at <https://noticias.uol.com.br/politica/eleicoes/2018/noticias/2018/10/08/mulheres-sao-15-do-novo-congresso-mas-indice-ainda-e-baixo.htm>.

On the spending in the 2018 elections, see 'Gastos de campanha chegaram a R$2 bilhões nas eleições 2018', *Varela Notícias*, 29 October 2018, at <http://varelanoticias.com.br/gastos-de-campanha-chegaram-a-r-2-bilhoes-nas-eleicoes-2018/>.

On growth during the Lula years see World Bank, GDP growth (annual %)—Brazil, at <https://data.worldbank.org/indicator/NY.GDP.MKTP.KD.ZG?locations=BR>.

Brazil's Truth Commission Report can be found at <http://cnv.memoriasreveladas.gov.br/>.

The data on homicides are from the Brazilian Forum for Public Security, Public Security in Numbers 2018, at <http://www.forumseguranca.org.br/wpcontent/uploads/2019/02/Infografico_an12_atualizado.pdf>.

On Brazil's prison population, see 'Highest to Lowest—Prison Population Total', at World Prison Brief, at <http://www.prisonstudies.org/highest-to-lowest/prison-population-total?field_region_taxonomy_tid=All>.

The estimate of people living under *milícias* in Rio de Janeiro comes from 'Franquia do crime: 2 milhões de pessoas no RJ estão em áreas sob control de milícias', 14 March 2018, available at <https://g1.globo.com/rj/rio-de-janeiro/noticia/franquia-do-crime-2-milhoes-de-pessoas-no-rj-estao-em-areas-sob-influencia-de-milicias.ghtml>.

The information on the proportion of the most violent cities in the world that were in Brazil in 2017 comes from Wendy Hunter and Timothy Power, 'Bolsonaro and Brazil's Illiberal Backlash', *Journal of Democracy*, Volume 30, Number 1, January 2019, pp. 68–82, citation on p. 73.

On populism, I use the definition that it is a 'thin-centred ideology that considers society to be ultimately separated into two homogeneous and antagonistic camps, "the pure people" versus "the corrupt elite", and which argues that politics should be an expression of the volonté general ("general will" of the people)'. From Cas Mudde and Cristóbal Rovira Kaltwasser, *Populism: A Very Short Introduction* (Oxford: Oxford University Press, 2017), p. 6.

On *The Intercept* reporting, see Glen Greenwald, Betsy Reed, and Leandro Demori, 'Como e por que o Intercept está publicando chats privados sobre a Lava Jato e Sérgio Moro', 9 June 2019, at <https://theintercept.com/2019/06/09/editorial-chats-telegram-lava-jato-moro/>.

On the resignation of Sérgio Moro from the Bolsonaro administration, see Guilherme Mazieiro, 'Moro sai e acusa Bolsonaro de inteferência política e ignorar carta branca', *UOL*, 24 April 2020, at <noticias.uol.com.br/politica/ultimas-noticias/2020/04/24/moro-demissao-ministerio-governo-bolsonaro.htm>.

On the military ministers and lower-level appointments, see Humberto Trezzi, 'Quem são e que cargos ocupam os militares no governo Bolsonaro', *Gaúchazh Política*, 9 February 2019, at <https://gauchazh.clicrbs.com.br/politica/noticia/2019/02/quem-sao-e-que-cargos-ocupam-os-militares-no-governo-bolsonaro-cjrwm3z6w027901tdxl16reku.html> and Maria Hermínia Tavares de Almeida, 'Perigo no terceiro piso', *Folha de São Paulo*, 20 February 2020, at <www.folha.com.br>.

On Eduardo Bolsonaro's comments on AI-5, see Guilherme Mazui, 'Eduardo Bolsonaro diz que, "se esquerda radicalizar", resposta "pode ser via um novo AI-5"', *O Globo*, 31 October 2019, at <https://g1.globo.com/politica/noticia/2019/10/31/eduardo-bolsonaro-diz-que-se-esquerda-radicalizar-resposta-pode-ser-via-um-novo-ai-5.ghtml#>.

On the views on gender equality of Minister Damares Alves, see 'Damares acredita que a igualdade de gênero estimula violência', *Cataraca Livre*, 8 March 2019, at <https://catracalivre.com.br/cidadania/damares-acredita-que-a-igualdade-de-genero-estimula-violencia/>. For her views on abortion see Natália Portinari, 'Com apoio de Damares, deputados re-lançam frente "pró-vida" que é contra aborto em todos as situações', *O Globo*, 27 March 2019, at

<https://oglobo.globo.com/sociedade/com-apoio-de-damares-deputados-relancam-frente-pro-vida-que-contra-aborto-em-todas-as-situacoes-23554191>.

On the investigation into Flávio Bolsonaro see 'Flávio Bolsonaro lavou até R\$1,6 milhão em loja de chocolate, diz Ministério Público', *Folha de São Paulo*, 19 December 2019, at <https://www1.folha.uol.com.br/poder/2019/12/flavio-bolsonaro-lavou-ate-r-16-milhao-em-loja-de-chocolate-diz-ministerio-publico.shtml>

On the international controversy over fires in the Amazon see Anthony Pereira, 'Amazon fires: Jair Bolsonaro faces mounting political backlash in Brazil—even from his allies', in *Politics Means Politics*, 29 August 2019, at <https://vip.politicsmeanspolitics.com/2019/08/28/amazon-fires-jair-bolsonaro-faces-mounting-political-backlash-in-brazil-even-from-his-allies/>.

On the firing of Health Minister Luiz Henrique Mandetta, see Clara Cerioni, `Após semanas de conflitos, Bolsonaro demite Mandetta', *Exame*, 16 April 2020, at <https://exame.abril.com.br/brasil/apos-semanas-de-conflitos-bolsonaro-demite-mandetta/>.

Chapter 7: Brazil and the multipolar world

The speech by Ernesto Araújo was found at <http://www.itamaraty.gov.br/pt-BR/discursos-artigos-e-entrevistas-categoria/ministro-das-relacoes-exteriores-discursos/19907-discurso-do-ministro-ernesto-araujo-durante-cerimonia-de-posse-no-ministerio-das-relacoes-exteriores-brasilia-2-de-janeiro-de-2019> and translated by the author.

The information on Josué de Castro is from Archie Davies, 'Josué de Castro's Geografia Combatente and the Political Ecology of Hunger' (London: Thesis submitted for a Ph.D. in Geography at King's College London, 2019).

About the letter from the ex-ministers of the environment, the source is Mauro Bellesa, 'Ex-ministros do meio ambiente condenam "desmonte da governança socioambiental"', Instituto de Estudos Avançados da Universidade de São Paulo, 8 May 2019, at <http://www.iea.usp.br/noticias/reuniao-ex-ministros-de-meio-ambiente>.

On the Amazon Fund, the data are from Fabíola Ortiz, 'Ten years on, Amazon Fund receives applause, criticism, faces new tests', *Mongabay*, 21 December 2018, at <https://news.mongabay.com/2018/12/ten-years-on-amazon-fund-receives-applause-criticism-faces-new-tests/>.

On the figure that 75 per cent of Brazil's electricity comes from
   hydroelectric sources, see Renewable Energy and Sustainability in
   Brazil, at <https://www.campusb.org/renewable-energy>.
On Minister Serra and the HIV-AIDS issue, the information is from
   'AIDS: vinte anos', at <http://www.joseserra.com.br/aids-vinte-
   anos/>, and 'Serra ameaça quebrar patente de remédio para a
   AIDS', at *BBC Brasil* 15 May 2001, <https://www.bbc.com/
   portuguese/noticias/2001/010515_serra.shtml>.
On religious nationalism see Mark Juergensmeyer,'The Global Rise of
   Religious Nationalism', *Australian Journal of International
   Affairs*, Volume 64, Number 3, June 2010, pp. 262–73.
On the Pentecostal share of the Brazilian electorate and their
   preference for Bolsonaro, see Wendy Hunter and Timothy Power
   (2019), pp. 68–82, citation on p. 77.

Chapter 8: Exuberance and diversity

The description of the Park of the City was based on personal
   observation by the author.
On Brazil's forest cover and being the country with more deforestation
   per year than any other, see Bernardo Esteves, 'O meio ambiente
   como estorvo', *Piauí* 153, Junho 2019, pp. 16–26; the citation is
   on p. 24.

Further reading

Chapter 1: Brazil hosts the Olympic Games

Boris Fausto and Sergio Fausto, *A Concise History of Brazil* (Cambridge: Cambridge University Press, second edition, 2014).

Gilberto Freyre, *The Masters and the Slaves: A Study in the Development of Brazilian Civilization* (New York: Alfred A. Knopf; translated by Samuel Putnam, 1946).

Jeffrey Garmany and Anthony Pereira, *Understanding Contemporary Brazil* (London: Routledge, 2018).

Stefan Zweig, *Brazil: A Land of the Future* (Riverside, Calif.: Ariadne Press, 2000).

Chapter 2: From colony to empire to republic

Lima Barreto, *The Sad End of Policarpo Quaresma* (London: Penguin Books, 2014).

Leslie Bethell, *The Abolition of the Brazilian Slave Trade: Britain, Brazil and the Slave Trade Question, 1807–1869* (Cambridge: Cambridge University Press, 1970).

Emília Viotti da Costa, *The Brazilian Empire: Myths and Histories* (Chapel Hill: University of North Carolina Press, revised edition, 2000).

Euclides da Cunha, *Revolt in the Backlands* (London: Gollancz; translated by Samuel Putnam, 1947).

John Hemming, *Red Gold: The Conquest of the Brazilian Indians* (Cambridge, Mass.: Harvard University Press, 1978).

Kenneth Maxwell, *Conflicts and Conspiracies: Brazil and Portugal 1750–1808* (New York: Routledge, 2004).

Chapter 3: The Vargas era and its legacy

Leslie Bethell, ed., *The Cambridge History of Latin America*. Volume IX: *Brazil Since 1930* (Cambridge: Cambridge University Press, 2008).

Florestan Fernandes, *The Negro in Brazilian Society* (New York: Columbia University Press, 1969).

Carolina Maria de Jesus, *Child of the Dark: The Diary of Carolina Maria de Jesus* (New York: Signet, 2003).

Robert M. Levine, *Father of the Poor? Vargas and his Era* (Cambridge: Cambridge University Press, 1998).

Karl Loewenstein, *Brazil Under Vargas* (New York: The MacMillan Company, 1942).

Laurence Whitehead, 'State Organisation in Latin America Since 1930', in Leslie Bethell, ed., *The Cambridge History of Latin America*, Volume VI, Part II (Cambridge: Cambridge University Press, 2008), pp. 1–95.

Chapter 4: Dictatorship and repression

Maria Helena Moreira Alves, *State and Opposition in Military Brazil* (Austin: University of Texas Press, 1988).

Christopher *Dunn, Brutality Garden: Tropicália and the Emergence of a Brazilian Counterculture* (Chapel Hill: University of North Carolina Press, 2001).

Anthony W. Pereira, *Political (In)justice: Authoritarianism and the Rule of Law in Brazil, Chile, and Argentina* (Pittsburgh: University of Pittsburgh Press, 2005).

Thomas Skidmore, *The Politics of Military Rule in Brazil 1964–85* (Oxford: Oxford University Press, 1990).

Alfred Stepan, *The Military in Politics: Changing Patterns in Brazil* (Princeton: Princeton University Press, 2015).

Alfred Stepan, *Rethinking Military Politics: Brazil and the Southern Cone* (Princeton: Princeton University Press, 1988).

Chapter 5: Rich country, poor people: economic challenges

Lee Alston, Marcus André Melo, Bernardo Mueller, and Carlos Pereira, *Brazil in Transition: Beliefs, Leadership and Institutional Change* (Princeton: Princeton University Press, 2016).

Tereza Campello, Tiago Falcão, and Patricia Vieira da Costa, eds, *Brazil Without Extreme Poverty* (Brasília: Ministry of Social Development and the Fight Against Hunger, 2015).

Alfredo Saad-Filho and Lecio Morais, *Brazil: Neoliberalism versus Democracy* (London: Pluto Press, 2018).

Ben Ross Schneider, *New Order and Progress: Development and Democracy in Brazil* (Oxford: Oxford University Press, 2016).

Chapter 6: Democratic development or decay?

Perry Anderson, *Brazil Apart: 1964–2019* (London: Verso, 2019).

Leonardo Avritzer, *Participatory Institutions in Democratic Brazil* (Baltimore: Johns Hopkins University Press, 2009).

James Holston, *Insurgent Citizenship: Disjunctions of Democracy and Modernity in Brazil* Princeton: Princeton University Press, 2009).

Wendy Hunter and Timothy J. Power, 'Bolsonaro and Brazil's Illiberal Backlash', *Journal of Democracy*, Volume 30, Number 1, January 2019, pp. 68–82.

Peter Kingstone and Timothy Power, eds, *Democratic Brazil Divided* (Pittsburgh: University of Pittsburgh Press, 2017).

Eduardo Mello and Matias Spektor, 'Brazil: The Costs of Multiparty Presidentialism', *Journal of Democracy*, Volume 29, Number 2, April 2018, pp. 113–27.

Chapter 7: Brazil and the multipolar world

Celso Amorim, *Acting Globally: Memoirs of Brazil's Assertive Foreign Policy* (Falls Village, Conn.: Hamilton Books, 2017).

Sean Burges, *Brazil in the World: The International Relations of a South American Giant* (Manchester: University of Manchester Press, 2017).

Celso Lafer, 'Brazil and the World', in Ignacy Sachs, Jorge Wilheim, and Paulo Sergio Pinheiro, eds, *Brazil: A Century of Change* (Chapel Hill: University of North Carolina Press 2009), pp. 101–19.

David Mares and Harold Trinkunas, *Aspirational Power: Brazil on the Long Road to Global Influence* (Washington DC: Brookings Institution Press, 2016).

Carlos Milani, Leticia Pinheiro, and Maria Regina Soares de Lima, 'Brazil's Foreign Policy and the "Graduation Dilemma"', *International Affairs*, Volume 93 Number 3, 2017, pp. 585–605.

Matias Spektor, 'Brazil: Shadows of the Past and Contested Ambitions', in William I. Hitchcock and Jeffrey W. Legro, eds, *Shaper Nations: Strategies for a Changing World* (Cambridge, Mass.: Harvard University Press, 2016), pp. 85–130.

Chapter 8: Exuberance and diversity

Roberto Da Matta, *Carnivals, Rogues and Heroes: An Interpretation of the Brazilian Dilemma* (Notre Dame, Ind.: University of Notre Dame Press, 1991).

Darcy Ribeiro, *The Brazilian People: The Formation and Meaning of Brazil* (Gainesville: University Press of Florida, 2000).

Thomas Skidmore, *Brazil: Five Centuries of Change* (Oxford: Oxford University Press, second edition, 2010).

Index

For the benefit of digital users, indexed terms that span two pages (e.g., 52–53) may, on occasion, appear on only one of those pages.

Index

Modern Brazil